# Sandplay Studies

*Contributing Authors*

Katherine Bradway
Karen A. Signell
Geraldine H. Spare
Charles T. Stewart
Louis H. Stewart
Clare Thompson

# Sandplay Studies
## *Origins, Theory and Practice*

Sigo Press

BOSTON

Originally published by the C.G. Jung Institute of San Francisco, 1981

SIGO PRESS
25 New Chardon Street # 8748
Boston, Massachusetts 02114

Publisher and Editor-in-Chief: Sisa Sternback

International Standard Book Number: 0-938434-40-3 (cloth)
    0-938434-41-1 (paperback)
Library of Congress Cataloging in Publication Data
    Sandplay Studies

    Bibliography: p.
    Includes index
    1. Sandplay—Therapeutic use. 2. Play Therapy
    I. Bradway, Katherine
RC489.S25S26      1990      616.89'1653      88-15804

Printed in Korea

# Table of Contents

# Foreword

I am very pleased to learn that "Sandplay,"* which I introduced to the C.G. Jung Institute of San Francisco, has gained such a wide interest among psychotherapists, including those taking a more scientific approach to the psyche. In general, I like to encourage any type of research that is done with Sandplay. I am sure that new discoveries and other approaches than those I have experienced myself can prove helpful in alleviating the suffering of the patient, and this should be the therapist's primary motivation, above and beyond the development of new techniques and ideas.

When I went to London in 1956 to study her "World Technique" with Dr. Margaret Lowenfeld, my main interest was in this technique as an ideal medium to approach the child's unconscious. However, I soon discovered that when the patient, be it a child or an adult, constructs "worlds" at regular intervals, one can observe a process of development beginning to move, guided by the hidden unconscious totality. For there in the sandtray, when the patient begins the play, he submits himself to the law of the psyche which leads to the union of the opposites; for the decisive characteristic of Sandplay seems to be that it is in itself a mediator be-

---

*Frau Kalff's unique relationship to sandplay, as parent and namer, is reflected here not only philosophically but typographically, in her capitalizing the name itself. The editors are delighted to honor her choice.

tween the poles of the visible and the invisible. Another important and obvious polarity in Sandplay is that of body and mind. The picture is formed physically in the sand, so that we can say that the inner contents find physical form. Since the figures used in the sandtray are made in the material world, an unconscious content is immediately transformed in the conscious world, thereby giving the patient the experience of the transformative qualities of energies.

Among others, a preliminary condition for the unfolding of inner forces is what I call "a free and protected space" for the patient. It is the task of the therapist to create such a space, a space in which the patient feels completely free and accepted, protected by the therapist, who must recognize the limitations of the patient. In this protected situation, the analytical process progresses towards a union of opposites through the act of playing. I therefore gave this method the name "Sandplay." Dr. Lowenfeld, in recognition of this observation, agreed to it. The act of playing in the sand allows the patient to come near his own totality.

At a certain point the patient, through the sandplay, penetrates to that which we can recognize as an expression of the Self. With this, a psychic situation of inner space is achieved, which leads to a deeply moving, numinous experience and to contact with the transcendental or spiritual realm. The ego as the center of the conscious personality is relativized in the sense that it recognizes that it is contained within the Self.

This experience is the basis of an initial transformation of energies. In sand pictures that follow, it is first expressed on a primitive level. Scenes of the plant and animal world appear. Water and earth are in the foreground. The patient experiences an encounter with the lowest levels of the body. At this time we also find the emergence of the contrasexual elements, or soul-images, of the personality: in the male, the creative feminine aspect called *anima;* in the female, the masculine logos aspect called *animus.*

These are new creative forces that begin to have an effect. At this moment the dark, hidden aspects that belong to the sphere of the instincts and impulses are represented in sand pictures. The recognition of these forces leads to confrontation with them and, on another level, to the transformation of these energies. With the help of the awakening creativity, they give life a new direction.

This is, in brief, how I view the process as I have experienced it with my patients. In my experience, Sandplay constitutes in itself a method whereby the individuation process is lived through and expressed. I personally have never considered it an adjunct to verbal analysis, to be used only at certain points in the therapeutic process. When it is used as an adjunct to verbal analysis, it may very well further the therapeutic work, but I do not think it will lead to the same types of experience that I have seen to be possible through a continuing use of Sandplay as the main emphasis of the therapy. I hope to make clearer these insights I have gained, and am still discovering, in a future publication should time and circumstances allow it.

*Dora M. Kalff*
*Zollikon, Switzerland*
*October, 1980*

To
Clare Wright Thompson
May 1, 1912—November 10, 1980

# Preface to the Second Edition

This book had its origins in a spontaneous eruption of enthusiasm among the several contributors to the volume, who realized that they were in the forefront of a significant new development in the field of psychotherapy. Drawing on their own experience, they hoped to provide some guidance for other psychotherapists using sandplay. In view of the fact that a new edition of the book is now warranted, the original enthusiasm and the anticipation that others would find the book useful seem both amply confirmed. With the exception of some improvements in the illustrations, the book remains unchanged. The authors were of the opinion that although they would change some details if they were writing their chapters now, they were nevertheless willing to have the chapters included in this edition as they were originally written.

The eight years since the original publication of this book have seen a rapidly growing interest in sandplay. Among the signs of interest is the increasing number of clinics for children which are now routinely equipping a room for sandplay. Sandplay is also finding a place in hospitals with treatment programs for sexually abused children, children with severe burns, and terminally ill children. School psychologists are using it widely even though they may have to requisition a broom closet or utility room for their use; and its place as standard equipment in the consulting rooms of individual practitioners of psychotherapy is on the rise. In addition, new publications have appeared over the intervening years (see the updated bibliography).

A major sign of the worldwide interest in sandplay was the founding in 1985 of the International Society for Sandplay Therapy by Dora Kalff and a group of twelve sandplay therapists who had been trained by her and who had been meeting in an informal colloquium in Switzerland for the three preceding years. Most of these founding members are also members of the International Association for Analytical Psychology. Divisions of the International Society are being established in the various countries represented, which currently include England, Germany, Italy, Japan, Switzerland, and the United States.

Speaking for all the authors, we are gratified that the volume supported and published by the C.G. Jung Institute of San Francisco in 1981 is still in demand.

Katherine Bradway and Louis Stewart
San Francisco, May 1989

# Acknowledgements

The publisher wishes to thank the following individuals for their contributions to the original edition, under the editorial direction of Dr. Gareth Hill: Wanda McCaddon, Maureen O'Shea, Joan Alpert, Mary Hood, Ursula Egli, and Barbara McClintock.

Grateful acknowledgement is made to the following for permission to reprint copyrighted material:

*American Journal of Orthopsychiatry* and Professor Erik H. Erikson for quotations from "Sex Differences in the Play Configurations of Preadolescents," Volume 21, pp. 667-692, copyright 1951 by the American Orthopsychiatric Association, Inc.

Arno Press for quotations from *Floor Games* by H.G. Wells, reprinted by Arno Press, Inc., 1975.

International Universities Press, Inc., for quotations from *Discussions on Child Development,* Volume 4, by J.M. Tanner and B. Inhelder, copyright 1960.

C.G. Jung Foundation for Analytical Psychology for quotations from *The Child* by Erich Neumann, published by G.P. Putnam's Sons for the C.G. Jung Foudation for Analytical Psychology, Inc., copyright 1973.

W.W. Norton and Company, Inc., for quotations from *Play, Dreams and Imitation in Childhood* by Jean Piaget, published by W.W. Norton and Company, Inc., 1962.

Pantheon Books for quotations from *Memories, Dreams, Reflections* by C.G. Jung, edited by Aniela Jaffé, translated by Richard and Clara Winston, published by Pantheon Books, a Division of Random House, Inc., copyright 1961.

Pergamon Press for reproduction of plates from *The Lowenfeld Technique* by Laura Ruth Bowyer, published by Pergamon Press, 1970.

Princeton University Press for quotations from *The Collected Works of C.G. Jung,* edited by Herbert Read, Michael Fordham, Gerhard Adler, William McGuire; translated by R.F.C. Hull; volumes 5, 6, 7, 8, 9i and 9ii, Bollingen Series XX. For quotations from *The Origins and History of Consciousness* by Erich Neumann, translated by R.F.C. Hull, Bollingen Series XLII, copyright 1954.

# Sandplay and
# The C. G. Jung Institute
# of San Francisco

LOUIS H. STEWART

The papers in this book testify to the remarkable impact on the San Francisco Bay Area community of psychotherapists, in particular Jungian analysts, of a Jungian analyst from Zurich, Dora M. Kalff. Her influence goes back nearly two decades. In late 1961 Frau Kalff visited the United States to present to interested professionals her clinical experience in the use of the Lowenfeld World Technique with children and young adults. Her appearance in the San Francisco Bay Area was heralded by Dr. Renée Brand, a San Francisco Jungian analyst who had known Frau Kalff in Europe. She alerted Katherine Bradway, Chairman of the Joint Conference of Jungian Analysts of Northern and Southern California, who passed the word to Dr. Joseph Henderson, president of the Northern California contingent. He in turn suggested that Frau Kalff be invited to give a presentation of her work at the March, 1962 conference. Thus occurred what Dr. Henderson was to call the San Francisco Bay Area "epiphany" of Dora Kalff; and thus—in a spontaneous human chain reaction—has her influence spread over the years. Just after her warmly received presentation at the Joint Conference, Frau Kalff met in San Francisco with a group of enthusiastic analysts for further discussion of her work. By the time she left, an informal Dora Kalff Committee had sprung into being, to keep in touch with developments in sandplay and facilitate the use of sandplay in clinical practice.

From this propitious beginning there flowed a series of almost yearly invitations to Frau Kalff to lecture, give seminars and provide training sessions for individuals. Over the years her audiences grew rapidly in size and in enthusiasm and her influence spread widely. Today it is a major event in the Jungian community when she can be persuaded to appear in San Francisco. From even a partial list of Dora Kalff's major presentations in the Bay Area one can gain some idea of the scope of her lectures: in 1966 she was invited to present her clinical work to the Children's Service of the San Mateo County Mental Health Services, then headed by Dr. Charles Stewart; during the same visit she presented a seminar at the C. G. Jung Institute in San Francisco, and in addition gave an evening lecture under the auspices of the Analytical Psychology Club of San Francisco. In 1969 and again in 1970 she was one of a distinguished group of Jungian analysts, writers and other creative individuals who provided two memorable weekends of lecture and discussion, arranged jointly by Drs. James Yandell and Harold Stone at the University of California in Berkeley, on the subjects "Fantasy, Dreams and Myths" and "The Forgotten Feminine." Dora Kalff's contributions were entitled "The Creative Imagination and the Development of the Child" and "Images of Renewal." In 1973 the C. G. Jung Institute and the Analytical Psychology Club jointly sponsored a Dora Kalff lecture at Lone Mountain College entitled "The Meditation of the Inner Fire"; and in 1974 at the University of California Medical Center Frau Kalff lectured and showed her film Sandplay, which demonstrates her actual work with children. In her most recent visit, in the Spring of 1979, she presented a lecture with clinical material entitled "Sandplay: Its Relation to Religion and the Feminine," again under the joint auspices of the C. G. Jung Institute and the Analytical Psychology Club.

There is, in addition to her lectures, another way in which Dora Kalff's presence has stimulated sandplay development in the Bay Area: through the coincidence of her visits to San Francisco with the gestation of the James Goodrich Whitney Clinic of the C. G. Jung Institute of San Francisco. The first proposal for a clinic to provide Jungian analysis and psychotherapy to the public at reduced fees had been made by Dr. James Whitney in the Fall of 1961 at a meeting of the Society of Jungian Analysts of Northern California. Within three years the C. G. Jung Institute was established with the express purpose of supporting such a clinic in addition to its other functions of public education, research and the training of Jungian analysts. As soon as the Institute was housed (in an old Victorian house on Clay Street) plans went ahead to open the clinic, conceived as having both service and research functions. By the time it was possible to begin seeing clients, Dora Kalff's presentations had convinced us that the clinic should have a room equipped for sandplay which could serve for both therapy and research. As co-director of the clinic with Dr. Melvin Kettner, I was assigned the enviable task of collecting the miniatures and equipping the sandplay room. In the Fall of 1966 Dr. Katherine Bradway saw the first clients in the sandplay room and we obtained from clinic intake procedures the first in a series of sand worlds.

Since then the sandplay room has seen good service in both therapy and research. Many analysts and candidates have made use of the equipment in their work with clinic patients, and it has been a useful adjunct to seminars in the training program of the Institute. Currently there are psychological interns who are learning to use the technique as part of their internship experience in the clinic. And finally the slow process of accumulation and analysis of research data has begun to bear fruit. Studies are now under way using the sand worlds and other psychological data in an investigation of the categories of the imagination and stages of ego development.

It is impossible to capture in words the qualities of Dora Kalff that captivated and inspired so many now-enthusiastic sandplay therapists. But while writing this history of her sojourns among us, I have found myself experiencing periodic waves of nostalgia, as well as vignettes of memories, my own and those of others with whom I have talked. As I try to distill these recollections into a clear impression there come to mind the words "a free and sheltered space," an expression which Dora Kalff coined to characterize the therapeutic atmosphere she seeks to foster in her work.

And this, it seems to me, is the best description of the effect she achieves as an individual and in her roles as teacher and psychotherapist. Her persuasive impact also resides in the sand worlds themselves. Even when frozen in the static images of slides projected upon a screen, they still retain some of the magical quality of the living worlds which were animated by the imagination of client and therapist alike, and which spring to life once again for all who can see them with the inner vision of imagination.

# Variations on a Theme by Lowenfeld: Sandplay in Focus

CLARE THOMPSON

## I
## Sandplay Is Born

As the present volume attests, sandplay is a very individual matter and is used differently by every therapist. Consequently, perhaps it can best be understood against the background of how, and through whom, it evolved.

The first date upon which there is general agreement is 1911 when H. G. Wells's book *Floor Games* was published in England; an American edition followed the next year. In this delightful book, recently republished* (Wells, 1975), Wells tells of activities in which he and his two sons participated. Though in terms of the development of sandplay a gestation period of 18 years lay ahead, many of its essential elements are described by Wells. Equipped with pieces of wood, paper, plasticine, and miniatures of people and animals, he and his sons engaged in protracted and elaborate floor games, one of which was the building of cities, another "wonderful islands." Wells's contribution to the field was not only in recognizing suitable materials, but in honoring the activity of creative imagination. For example, in describing the building of a castle he says: "Of course, it goes without saying that we despise those foolish, expensive, made-up wooden and pasteboard castles that are sold in shops—playing with them is like playing with

---

*New York: Arno Press. Page citations throughout refer to this edition.

somebody else's dead game in a state of *rigor mortis*" (p. 23). The essential characteristic of his book is its liveliness—the liveliness of sandplay itself.

The next principal to appear on the scene was Margaret Lowenfeld, who started her long professional life as an English pediatrician. In 1925 she left orthodox pediatrics and began the psychiatric treatment of children. At that time she remembered *Floor Games,* published "in my youth," when she was twenty-one. "I collected first a miscellaneous mass of material, colored sticks and shapes, beads, small toys of all sorts, paper shapes and matchboxes, and kept them in what came to be known by my children as the 'Wonder Box'" (Lowenfeld, 1979, p. 3).

In 1929 she moved her child clinic, later to be called The Institute of Child Psychology (ICP), to new quarters and added new features to the playroom equipment. Among these were two zinc trays placed on tables, one filled with sand and one with water. This was not the first introduction of such equipment into a playroom, but what developed from it makes it remarkable. The "Wonder Box," of course, was part of the playroom equipment, its miniature models of ordinary people and objects now housed in the small drawers of an old birds' egg collection cabinet which stood upon one of the playroom tables. Now the children came to call this cabinet "the world."

During the first month in the newly equipped playroom a child combined some of the miniatures and the sand-filled tray, and within two more months workers writing up case notes were referring to the constructions in the sandtray (by now a common event) as "worlds." Ville Andersen reports: "Less than three months after a metal tray with moldable sand placed on a table, and a cabinet containing small miniature objects were included in the playroom equipment, a spontaneous new technique had developed *created by the children themselves*" (Bowyer, 1970, p. 8).

Almost fifty years later a friend, aware of my interest in sandtray worlds, wrote to me from the University of Oregon Health Sciences Center:

My students do play therapy of the more conventional sort, of course; but in the playroom is a sandbox. (Except we use cornmeal instead of sand so that tiny and/or retarded children can eat it more safely). But the playroom is otherwise equipped with the usual things—families of dolls, doll houses, animal figures, etc. And big things—Bobo's and balls and blocks. But it is fascinating to me that *all* the kids, sooner or later, bring the figures (which are on a table across the room) to the cornmeal box and set them up in the cornmeal and play with them there, exactly as if they *need* a sand-tray, and this is the best substitute they can find. (Garner, Note 1)

One of the original goals Lowenfeld set herself in designing her child clinic was "to find a medium which would in itself be instantly attractive to children and which would give them and the observer a 'language,' as it were, through which communication could be established" (Lowenfeld, 1979, p. 281). One should note that she says "to find a medium," not "to design a medium," for as Ville Andersen points out, "... the foundation of the whole concept of the treatment of children was that if given the right tools they would find their way to communication of their interior experience" (Ibid, p. 281).

The spontaneity—the inevitability, almost—which characterized the development of sandplay is to my mind its best validation as a method of communication.

The basic elements of what Lowenfeld came to call the "World Technique" have remained virtually unchanged since its beginning in 1929. These elements, like those of sandplay, are imaginative activity with sand, used with or without objects, within a circumscribed space, in the presence of a therapist.

Lowenfeld's first important paper on the topic was published in 1939, but she had demonstrated the method at various international congresses as early as 1937. A Swiss Jungian child analyst, Dora Kalff, attended such a congress in Switzerland where two "worlds" were exhibited. She recognized that she must make this method her own and went to London to study with Lowenfeld in 1956. Returning to Zurich she continued consulting with Jung, who, together with his late wife Emma, had been largely responsible for her analytic training and career. Though it is a matter of record that Jung had attended the Eleventh International Congress of Psychology in Paris in 1937 and interpreted one of Lowenfeld's worlds there, Kalff reports that, twenty years later, he made no mention of this. Jung's own "building game," in which he erected a village on the shore of Lake Zurich, is sometimes seen as a forerunner of sandplay (L. Stewart, 1977, p. 9), though Kalff does not agree. She does agree, however, that Jung was a most helpful consultant in developing her own method of sandplay—the name she gives it.

In 1962 Kalff gave a paper at the Second International Congress of Analytical Psychology and caught the imagination of many Jungian analysts. Though she has surprisingly few publications on the topic of sandplay, she has taught and lectured widely on it with such effectiveness that in some places (San Francisco, for example) the professional community looks on sandplay as something exclusively Jungian. Indeed I know of no Jungian using the method who has not been introduced to it either directly or indirectly by Kalff. In turn, Kalff has acknowledged her debt to Lowenfeld: "She understood completely the child's world and created with ingenious intuition a way which enables the child to build a world—his world—in a sandbox" (Kalff, 1971, p. 32).

At about the same time as Lowenfeld, though independently, Melanie Klein also introduced the idea of play in child therapy. So far as the orientation of this paper is concerned, Klein is most important for her influence on Winnicott, who in turn has been important to Michael Fordham, the London child analytical psychologist. In fact, Alfred Plaut, former editor of the Journal of Analytical Psychology, dubbed the Fordham group of which he is a member a "Jung-Klein-hybrid" (quoted in Henderson, 1975, p. 198).

My own interests have led me to follow the Kleinian developments mainly for their influence on Erik Erikson, whose work on preadolescent play (Erikson, 1951) I see as the most compelling illustration of how a method such as sandplay can lead through observation to meaningful theories. Both Erikson and Lowenfeld approached the method empirically to see where it would lead them. For Erikson, it led to a whole new psychoanalytic formulation of women (Erikson, 1964). For Lowenfeld the outcome was a systematic understanding of the "thinking" of children.

Before 1933, Lowenfeld had been in correspondence with Charlotte Bühler, whose methods of infant observation she admired. In 1934 Bühler came to London and organized an institute for the study of normal children, where Lowenfeld's students as well as her own were able to study. Bühler visited ICP and watched children making worlds. She became interested in cross-cultural research and in standardization for use as a diagnostic test. Interrupted by the second world war, contact between Lowenfeld and Bühler did not resume until the nineteen fifties, by which time their developments had diverged widely. Various normative studies are for instance more closely related to Bühler's work than to Lowenfeld's.

In this connection, one should mention the work of Hedda Bolgar and Liselotte Fischer (1947) in obtaining normative data on adults who were educationally and socio-economically somewhat superior. Another offshoot of Bühler's work was the development of the Village Test by French psychologists (Mucchielli, Note 2; Paterson, Note 3). Conceptually very similar to the world technique, this test has advantages for certain situations and has led to some useful thinking. Since my own interests have led me to pursue only the therapeutic use of the sandtray, however, standardization will not be part of the survey in this chapter; the interested reader is referred to the bibliography in the appendix.

Developing from many sources, as we have seen, the sandplay method has always, for every innovator, begun with children, but I know of no avenue which has not led to its use with adults as well. Possibly the first to extend it to young adults was Erikson in his 1937 work with Harvard students (Homburger, 1938). In a 1939 lecture Lowenfeld, when questioned, referred to its use with a nineteen-year-old. Kalff's mothers, as she tells us in her film, became interested in sandplay through the work of their children, and it is now an important part of her analytic work with adults.

And in her 1979 book, Lowenfeld describes the method as being independent of age. She includes a chapter on "On the Subjective Making of a World," describing material which can be secured only from adults, not from children. In general, therapists who see both children and adults and who use the sandtray in their work do not judge its appropriateness on the basis of age, but on other grounds.

# II
# Methodology

A technique created by children is to be used with awe and wonder—certainly not with rigidity. But it is characteristic of people who write on this subject to sound very rigid indeed. The size of the tray, for example, is specified to the half inch or centimeter, and instructions foɪ the world-maker are frequently spelled out so exactly that it is obviously impossible to adhere to them in actual practice. But who told the children who invented world-making what to do?

The best evidence about the importance—or rather the unimportance—of instructions comes from Erikson. In the nineteen thirties he presented Harvard students with a collection of toys and blocks from which to create a scene. The subject "was told that the observer (who was unknown to him) was interested in ideas for moving picture plays and wished him to use the toys to construct on a second table a *dramatic scene*" (Homburger, 1938, pp. 553-4). "*Five out of the twenty-two* subjects ignored the instructions. . . . Of the remaining seventeen subjects only *four* constructed dramatic scenes which were not automobile accidents." Of these results Erikson (1951, p. 669) says, "The Harvard students were all English majors educated in the imagery of the finest in English drama. But they were observed to build scenes of remarkably *little dramatic* flavor."

In a second large-scale research project (Erikson, 1951, p. 668), preadolescent girls and boys were told: "I am interested in moving pictures. . . . Of course, I could not provide you with a real studio and real actors and actresses; you will have to use these toys instead. Choose any of the things you see here and construct on this table an *exciting* scene out of an *imaginary* moving picture. Take as much time as you want and tell me afterward what the scene is about." Of the results he obtained here Erikson (1951, p. 670) reports: "The children of this study produced scenes with a striking lack of similarity with movie clichés. In nearly 500 constructions, not more than three were compared with actual moving pictures. In no case was a particular doll referred to as representing a particular actor or actress. Lack of movie experience can hardly be blamed for this; the majority of these children attended movies regularly and had their favorite actors and types of pictures."

Such studies illustrate the lack of correspondence between the instructions to and the behavior of the world-maker. Looking back at the original authors of the method—the uninstructed children themselves—one sees that minimal instructions are in fact needed. In my own use of sandplay, I keep it as nonverbal as possible.

But the extent to which each therapist prescribes procedure, to world-makers or to the profession, will naturally depend on his or her general therapeutic viewpoint. For it needs emphasizing here that sandplay, however useful and exciting, is not a treatment in itself but an adjunct to treatment, and the approach to it *must* vary with the individual therapist. In my opinion we cannot remind ourselves of this often enough.

My own research, in the interests of this paper, into the "proper" measurements of the sandtray revealed a situation closely allied to chaos; Louis Stewart's (1977, p. 9) prescription of "approximately 30 × 20 × 3 inches" is a median; there is no mode.

Discussions of sandtray size almost always assume that one is, of course, talking about a rectangular tray. Yet Erikson used a square table. Albino (1954, p. 62), reporting that "The world game of Lowenfeld (1939) was chosen as the most appropriate technique for this study" (of defenses against aggression), goes on to to say, "The tray was circular instead of rectangular," but does not explain why or discuss the effect of the shape. Kamp and Kessler (Note 4) used a specially made table with one rounded end, rather like a household ironing board. This was designed to provide data on their impression that some children follow the outline of a table in placing their items. Unfortunately, their manuscript is unpublished and Bowyer's (1970, pp. 82-84) report does not comment on findings related to the shape.

The height of the sandtray above the floor is another dimension about which therapists differ widely. At least in her early work, Kalff used a uniform height for all world-makers. On the other hand she thought it important that the whole scene be observable without moving the head, which seems impossible with a single height for everyone. Lowenfeld's last specification was that the sandtray be waist high. I myself hoped, unsuccessfully, to find a mechanism like that on a barber's chair, whereby each individual could find his own preferred height. A similar end might be served by a series of drawer-like trays in a cabinet. One sandplay therapist I know has trays at a variety of heights; because she sees many preschool children, her lowest one is designed for them, but it was used by an adult woman who knelt to make a tray. Karen Signell,* on the other hand, tells us that she places the tray on the floor "similar to the way we played as children."

In general, people who work with the sandtray agree that the miniatures should be grouped in some way according to categories. But in the similar Village Test the miniatures are dumped before the subject, and the need to make order out of chaos is seen as an important aspect of the procedure. R. W. Pickford uses the world material in the same way (Bowyer, 1970, p. 17).

Miniatures are usually classified in eight categories: buildings; trees and bushes; fences and gates; wild animals; domestic animals; transport; people; and multi-purpose materials such as string, plas-

---

*Karen A. Signell, "The Use of Sandplay with Men," this volume p. 101.

ticine and paper. A recent seven-page list drawn up by the London ICP group includes these categories, but also spells out the inclusion of "phantasy animals" and, under "people," of "phantasy and folk-lore figures." Outer space has also become a category. Sets of miniatures, such as Britain's Model Farm Animals and Zoo Animals, are carefully scaled: for example, the giraffe is 5⅝ inches and the rabbit ⅜ of an inch tall. A variety of scale, on the other hand, affords the possibility of expressing psychological importance or dominance, or of expressing distance through perspective.

Lowenfeld prefers that the materials be arranged in drawers, so that the child has control of the amount and kind of stimulation to which he is exposed at any one time. Kalff uses shelves (photographed in her 1971 book, p. 35), as do most of her students. Robert Royeton, a Lowenfeld student, uses a combination of drawers and shelves. I control the danger of the subject's being overwhelmed by arranging the sandtable so that the world-maker has the material on shelves at his back except when he chooses purposively to face it to find objects.

The importance of having these shelves or cabinets in the consulting room itself depends upon how therapists see the method as integrating into their work. Some offices seem dominated by a sandtray; in others the equipment is in a separate room. I am indebted to a fellow therapist for the design I use: a cabinet five feet high and eight feet wide, with double doors which open and swing back to expose sixteen-foot shelves running across the inside of each door and the back of the cabinet. When they are shut, the decorative wooden doors form part of the office decor. To this I have added an étagère, on the shelves of which are displayed shells, stones, driftwood, and other natural objects. When the cabinet doors are open, these latter objects are available for sandplay. They are also used during more traditional analysis; one or both of us, for instance, may caress a stone or a bit of driftwood during a session. Again, this étagère and its contents add to the decor of the office.

All sandplay therapists agree that recording is important. Just how it should be done, on the other hand, is debated. Probably the

most frequently used method is photography. The obvious dif-
ficulty here is that if a shot is taken straight down into the sandtray,
any molding of the sand is lost; if it is taken from any other angle,
some of the foreground is cut off by the side of the tray. I ask the
world-maker to take a Polaroid print that best captures the scene
he or she meant to make; then we take a 35mm slide from the
same angle. There is, of course, no rule limiting the photographer
to only one angle. Lowenfeld and others find diagrams preferable,
and the illustrations in her book offer a good argument for this
method. Aite (1978) gives both a color photograph and a diagram,
a combination that clearly illustrates the advantages of each. Erikson went from photographs to schematic sketches, for which he
marked his table off in squares.

The purpose of recording naturally varies with the purpose of
the sandplay. Lowenfeld wanted to study the thinking of her children. Erikson wanted to use his constructions for comparison
with other data. Kalff, and most of her students, review the course
of therapy with the analysand by reviewing a series of sandtray
slides. Or such records can be used to check a clinical hunch about
groups of people: what characterizes boys as different from girls,
adolescents as different from children, or the people one is seeing
now as different from those one saw fifteen years ago? Lowenfeld
points out that consultation is an additional reason for recording:
other psychotherapeutic data brought to the consultant have been
already processed through the psyche of the therapist; a slide has
not. Most people who consult with me about their sandtray work ·
with their own patients, for example, do so by bringing in slides.
Even when we reconstruct the actual scene in my sandtray, the
slide is an invaluable aid.

One seems to have to learn for oneself how to balance the need
for a record against the primacy of the therapeutic process. This
problem goes back to the very beginning of the method. Though
his aim was not therapeutic, Wells makes the same point (1911/
1975, pp. 76-78). "As I wanted to photograph the particular set-
out for the purpose of illustrating this account, I took a larger share
in the arrangement than I usually do. It was necessary to get every-

thing into the picture, to ensure a light background. . . . When the photographing was over, matters became more normal. I left the schoolroom and when I returned I found that the group of rifle-men which had been converging on the public house had been sharply recalled to duty." Eickhoff (1952, p. 241) confesses at one point to "My secret zeal for photography having outrun temporar-ily my therapeutic sense." Of course, a discrepancy between the therapist's needs and the therapeutic needs is not specific to the sandtray. Although I was not aware of it at the time, it was proba-bly such a consideration that led me in my own work to involve the world-maker so fully in the recording process.

Constructions do not always stay the same, and recording com-plements and enhances therapeutic movement. During the past year I have been struck by a few cases in which the world-maker found it essential to change a construction with which he or she had been pleased at the time of making it. In each case, the changes took the form of simplification: extraneous parts of the world had to go. The record of each step in this process, as well as a review of inner and outer events at the various times, was essential for the world-maker to incorporate the experience.

In dream work it is my practice that both the analysand and I have copies of the dreams. In sandtray work I vary this by retain-ing all photographs of the sandtrays until one or both of us sees need for a review; after this review, the analysand keeps one copy of each photograph. The decision that the time has come for re-view may be subjective, or it may be prompted by circum-stances—the termination of therapy, for example, or a temporary cessation which allows time to review material before beginning again. I frequently use such an opportunity for dream review also.

The order and method of world-making may also become a significant matter of record. Many sandtray therapists make a running account during the process, and Lowenfeld was of the opinion that the child experienced this as lending dignity and im-portance to his or her production. However, as a world-maker myself, I find this a distracting interference with the process; con-sequently as a therapist my notes are almost always made afterward and, as with the photographic recording, with the participation of the world-maker. Methods of sandplay therapists range from this degree of casualness or, indeed, from no recording at all, to the elaborate apparatus of Dahlgren (1957).

Another matter that needs recording is what the selected object means to the world-maker. Lowenfeld seems to have been meticulous in this regard. She describes herself as imagining with the child that she is a south sea islander who has never seen Europe, and having the child explain to her what each object actually is, "that is, is to him" (1979, p. 7). One is reminded of Jung's injunctions about associations of dream images, insights which are made even more available and understandable to us in a case discussed by Mary Ann Mattoon (1978, pp. 185-195). I especially like Lowenfeld's warning (1979) about the dangers of unverified assumptions:

> . . . a world-maker standing in front of an open drawer containing a number of representations of houses of different shapes and sizes "took up a medium sized house and put it on the flat sand in the world tray". . . . To the individual who has taken up the house it *may* represent "a house," but it may also and with equal possibility represent nothing of the sort. It may be the nearest object he can find to stand to him for the idea of "safety," of "being under observation," of "the restrictions of urban life," of "family," or simply a conveniently sized and shaped rectangular object he can use as a plinth later to put a horseman on to form a statue. (p. 255)

Assumptions about the meaning of objects and behavior can be very far off the mark. An example is the activity of burying, which is too easily seen as aggression. Bowyer (1959, p. 162) reports that children aged two to four tend to pour sand over people and objects in the sandtray. Moreover, "Sometimes the vigor of the young child prevents him from balancing an animal on the surface of the sand, or perhaps non-recognition of the surface boundary causes him to thrust objects deep into the sand." Bowyer reports that Eve Lewis wrote to her, "I have often observed the careful burying of some toy to indicate not aggression but the acceptance of that which the toy symbolizes in the collective unconscious. The child usually asks that it be left for him to find again next time" (1959, p. 162). Nor need the presence of wild animals signify aggression.

Even though I am aware of all this, the value I attach to the non-verbal character of the method leads me to avoid long verbal discussions in my own work. Again, I try to have the production experienced rather than analyzed away. As Jung says of the value of the dreaming process, so Lowenfeld (1950, p. 330) says of sandplay: "The mere fact of making a series of worlds, and having them recorded, in itself brings about amelioration in the disturbances and discomforts of some children."

On the other hand, the therapist may be aware of meanings and symbolism beyond those the world-maker offers, and these additional meanings have their own value, as in Jung's concept of amplification. For instance, Erikson's play constructions showed parallels between the houses built by preadolescent girls and the female body (Erikson, 1964), and in his earlier work on the subject he elaborated a similar observation with material which certainly qualifies as amplification:

> We use this metaphor consciously too. We speak of our body's "build"; and of the "body" of vessels, carriages and churches. In spiritual and poetic analogies, the body carries the connotation of an abode, prison, refuge, or temple inhabited by, well, ourselves: "This mortal house," as Shakespeare put it. Such metaphors, with varying abstractness and condensation, express groups of ideas which are sometimes too high, sometimes too low, for words. In slang, too, every outstanding part of the body, beginning with the "underpinnings," appears translated into metaphors of house parts. . . . Whatever this proves, it does show that it takes neither erudition nor a special flair for symbolism to understand these metaphors. (Erikson, 1951, p. 691)

The endless variations in methodology presented above will, I hope, give the therapist reader permission to approach sandplay in his own way.*

---

*This attitude finds support in Geraldine Spare's paper "Are There Any Rules? (Musings of a Peripatetic Sandplayer)," this volume p. 195.

# III
# A Point of View

Eickhoff (1952, p. 235) says, "The most therapeutically exciting and satisfying medium in my experience is the sandtray with its equipment. Here is plastic material in the shape of sand and water by means of which gross feelings can be expressed, for it can be thrown, tossed, molded, plastered, dug and smoothed; and on this basis concrete symbols can be placed so that a situation is very easily presented to the gazer." In this description she has listed many of the advantages of the medium.

Most writers agree that one of its advantages is the ease with which a situation can be presented; the sandtray requires no special skill, artistic or otherwise. It can be used by those with few language skills, notably the retarded and young children. The emphasis is on nonverbal communication—with one's self and with one's therapist—and Lowenfeld sees this as so important that she emphasizes it in the instructions she gives children. In my experience, this nonverbal quality has a Janus-headed advantage which I first noticed during my own experience as a world-maker. To do away with words is a benefit not only for the verbally inadequate but for the oververbal intellectual. For the first time I realized that in my many years of personal and training analysis, I had been using words to obscure—not only from my analysts but from myself. Returning from Zurich to an American college town, I found the nonverbal sandplay therapy method enthusiastically received by therapists of faculty and student-body.

And quite apart from the inadequate or overly adequate verbal ability of the world-maker, the nonverbal sandtray world enables the sandplayer to portray events on many levels at the same time—in the way they are presented in dreams. But in dream therapy, the dreamer must translate the dream images into words and must order them to be spoken serially. Lowenfeld (1979, pp. 16-24) gives an exposition of what she later called the "protosystem." She makes an analogy to "that mixture of fairy story and children's tale in which there was a garden surrounded by a wall which all the grown-ups took as being really the end of the garden. . . ." These pages of Lowenfeld are worth reading and digesting: she refers to experience in which there is "neither time nor space"—a phrase certainly reminiscent of Jung. Indeed I find that her whole "secret garden" theme parallels what a Jungian analyst (Spencer, 1979, pp. 55-58) calls sacred, as opposed to profane, time and space.

A second advantage of the sandtray is its delimited space, so that, as Kalff puts it, "the player's fantasy is bounded and held within limits" (1971, p. 23). This is also true of the tables used by Erikson and Klein. The delimited space is complementary to the freedom and protection offered by the latitude and containment of the therapeutic situation itself.

As I indicated above about therapeutic work in general, I beware of "analyzing the process away" and I would emphasize this in the use of sandplay therapy. Whereas it is gratifying to get more and more penetrating glimpses of how the process is working, the experience itself is the all important ingredient: the experience of oneself making worlds and the experience of being there for another world-maker. The kind of understanding required of the therapist in the latter situation is not an intellectual exercise but a "being with"—not qualitatively different from what occurs in therapeutic hours that do not involve the making of sandtray worlds.

Lowenfeld's objective (1979, p. 3) was "to help children to produce something which will stand by itself and be independent of any theory as to its nature." Most of the case material in the present volume is presented by Jungian analysts and reflects, as does everything else we do, our basic orientation. When one lives by symbols, then axiomatically one approaches the sandtray world through symbols. And one probably calls it by Kalff's word—sandplay.

Because the volume in which this paper appears is under the auspices of a Jung Institute, the interpretations offered here are from that point of view. For instance, I am constantly struck by how "Jungian" Lowenfeld's formulations seem, even though her objective was to arrive at them empirically. Her 1979 book, *The World Technique*, is strongly recommended.

But once again we must remind ourselves that the theory is a function of the therapist using the sandtray, not of the world method itself. Indeed, two of the most serious students of the sandtray, both of whom use it therapeutically, differ widely in theory: Bowyer (1970) finds Lewin's theory most helpful; Kamp follows Piaget (Kamp and Kessler, Note 4). "Toys to children are like culinary implements to the kitchen; every kitchen has them and has also the elements of food. It is what the cook does with these implements and elements that determines the dish" (Lowenfeld, 1979, p. 3). Quite different dishes are cooked by therapists all over the world.

Either from a Jungian-Kalffian point of view, or more widely seen as sandtray therapy, sandplay is a very personal affair. It evokes the whole self of the therapist—orientation, value-system, unconscious. Ann Bernhardt (Note 5) has called it an excellent way for analyst and analysand to connect on an unconscious level, for there is the analyst's unconscious spread out on the shelves. And it is only when the method is used as a "test" rather than a psychotherapeutic adjunct that a standard set of materials is used.

In her article "The Versatility of the World Technique," Ruth Pickford (1973, p. 23) concludes, "The aim of this paper has been to encourage those who have not used the world technique to try it for their own purposes and so to experience for themselves its versatility." With slight variation my conclusion echoes hers: My hope is to encourage therapists of all persuasions to experience sandplay for themselves and to try it for their own purposes in whatever way is consonant with their general therapeutic approach.

# Play and Sandplay

LOUIS H. STEWART

## I
## Introduction

Sandplay as a vehicle of psychotherapy and Jungian analysis is rooted in the symbolic play of childhood, and can best be understood as an expression of the archetype of the child. In its origins, as the Lowenfeld world technique, it is naturally classified with the play therapies, where it has found a secure niche and a widespread appreciation among psychotherapists. As sandplay (from Dora Kalff's *Sandspiel*), the name it is generally known by among psychotherapists and analysts of a Jungian persuasion, it holds a special place as a paradigm of what Jung termed "active imagination," an activity which facilitates the process of individuation. Viewed from a historical perspective, in its evolution over the past century from its incipient beginnings in H. G. Wells's *Floor Games* (1911) to Margaret Lowenfeld's "world technique" (Lowenfeld, 1935), and thence to Dora Kalff's *Sandspiel* (1966), sandplay mirrors the mysterious presence of the Eternal Child playing his archetypal games, and slowly but surely bringing to consciousness a new awareness of the child within and the child archetype.

Sandplay is of course not the only indication of this revolution in modern consciousness. The International Year of the Child sponsored by UNESCO has just passed into history, and books can now be written about the history of childhood (Aries, 1962; deMause, 1974). But sandplay by its very nature, because it is "nothing but" the normal symbolic play of childhood, provides a pure "culture" for observation and places the psychotherapist in a unique and privileged position as a participant observer.

This remarkable development is worthy of serious study in its totality, but we shall confine ourselves here to what we may learn from sandplay itself. First we shall consider its material substance, the *prima materia,* the source of its power to evoke play and the creative imagination. Then we shall briefly recapitulate the migratory course sandplay has followed from its natural habitat in backyards and vacant lots into the home and clinic, and now into the offices of Jungian analysts where it has most recently taken up residence. This will bring us to a consideration of C. G. Jung's writings on the function of play in life and in psychotherapy, for as we shall see, in the final stage of its migration, sandplay reached a way station on Jung's doorstep. And it would appear that Jung himself prefigured sandplay in the course of the midlife "confrontation with the unconscious" which he relates in his memoirs (Jung, 1961, pp. 170-99) and through which he discovered the role of play and active imagination in the process of individuation.

# II

# The *Prima Materia*

Sandplay is one of those phenomena whose true nature and purpose are transparently visible in their substance. Its combination of sand and miniature toys juxtaposes natural elements which comprise the basic ingredients of childhood play. Children, everywhere, have always turned spontaneously to their native soil, and to the miniaturizing of the world about them, as fundamental tools with which to accomplish the indispensable early molding of their interior earth, the ground of their existence, and the structuring of the inner world of their imagination. The effectiveness of sandplay in clinic playrooms and in the offices of psychotherapists and analysts rests precisely on this fact, that it represents the archetypal elements of the spontaneous play of childhood, or what Jung called the third modality of the psyche, matter and spirit (Jung, 1972, par. 251).

We can see from the following examples just how serious a business such play is for children, a fact that often eludes us unless we can recapture our own early memories of digging to China, making mudpies, or reconstructing the world in replica. First, four-year-old children playing in the yard of a New York nursery school (Gould, 1972):

Chris: I hate women!

Teacher: Why do you say that, Chris?

Chris: Because when ya' marry them ya' hafta' get your blood tested.

Teacher: What else do you think about women, Chris?

Chris: I think they're kookie! I think I'm gonna marry a princess . . . because they're better—they're prettier.

Jim: Yeah, because they have jewels and gold—and they have crowns!

Olivia (comes over to the boys): What are you doing?

Jim and Chris: We're digging and looking for princesses.

. . .

Jim: Yeah, ya' don't find them in New York. We're digging our way to find one.

Chris: Well, ya' just don't marry one like the regular way. Ya' hafta' save one first. Princesses fall in love with princes.

. . .

Chris (running around the hole he has dug): Romance! (Running full circle again.) Princesses! (Running full circle a third time.) Jewels! Let's get digging for those princesses!

Jim: No, we don't really want them. We hafta' wait till we're grown up for that.

Chris: Yeah, till we're twenty-one!

Jim: Yeah.

Chris: And then we can buy a real drill and shovel and a pick.

Jim: And a whole car—and one of those things that go rrr-rrr-rrr.

Teacher: You mean a pneumatic drill?

Jim: Yeah. (pp. 22-23)

And now the open fields surrounding a distant village of stone age people in Western New Guinea, only recently discovered and not visited by outsiders until 1954. The examples are taken from a report of an anthropological expedition to the village in 1961 (Matthiessen, 1969).

> The one-eyed Aloka had retreated to the hill above before the funeral had ended. There, on a grassy knoll, singing to himself, the boy built a toy sili [a home enclosure] out of twigs and grass, complete with entrance way and fence. He hunched over it, content, staring and picking at what he had accomplished . . . [and another boy, Tukum,] alienated from the other boys went up to the hillside where . . . left to himself, he dug a long, deep burrow in a bank. Into this he placed an ear-shaped fungus he had found nearby. He packed it in with earth, then hiperi leaves and grass, then more earth, then more leaves, and so on, until the burrow was full. The fungus he called *mokat-asuk,* or ghost-ear, and his idea was that the mokut-asuk would listen for the return of his father, who is dead . . . [S]o far as is known, the ceremony of mokat-asuk is not an effective one, and is in fact, unknown to any of the Akuni, except Tukum. (pp. 205, 232)

Both our examples bear witness to the universality and the timelessness of this kind of play in childhood. Moreover, the last example brings to mind a similar event in the life of Jung which he has described in his memoirs (Jung, 1961):

> My disunion with myself and uncertainty in the world at large led me to an action which at the time was quite incomprehensible to me. I had in those days a yellow, varnished pencil case of the kind commonly used by primary-school pupils, with a little lock and the customary ruler. At the end of this ruler I now carved a little manikin, about two inches long, with frock coat, top hat, and shiny black boots. I colored him black with ink, sawed him off the ruler, and put him in the pencil case, where I made him a little bed. I even made a coat for him out of a bit of wool. In the case I also placed a smooth, oblong blackish stone from the Rhine, which I had painted with water colors to look as though it were divided into an upper and lower half, and had long carried around in my trouser pocket. This was *his* stone. All this was a great secret. Secretly I took the case to the forbidden attic at the top of the house

(forbidden because the floorboards were worm-eaten and rotten) and hid it with great satisfaction on one of the beams under the roof—for no one must ever see it! . . . I felt safe, and the tormenting sense of being at odds with myself was gone. In all difficult situations, whenever I had done something wrong or my feelings had been hurt, or when my father's irritability or my mother's invalidism oppressed me, I thought of my carefully bedded-down and wrapped-up manikin and his smooth, prettily colored stone. From time to time—often at intervals of weeks—I secretly stole up to the attic when I could be certain that no one would see me. Then I clambered up on the beam, opened the case, and looked at my manikin and his stone. Each time I did this I placed in the case a little scroll of paper on which I had previously written something during school hours in a secret language of my own invention. The addition of a new scroll always had the character of a solemn ceremonial act. (p. 21)

This type of play can hardly be called "playful." It is clearly ritualistic and carries religious overtones. In such "play" children are responding to the same dim impulses that have moved mankind from time immemorial to seek communication with the spirit world, the realm of the ancestors. Late in his life Jung (1961) said of his childhood ritual:

The meaning of these actions, or how I might explain them, never worried me. I contented myself with the feeling of newly won security, and was satisfied to possess something that no one could get at. . . . It was an inviolable secret which must never be betrayed, for the safety of my life depended on it. Why that was so I did not ask myself. It simply was so. . . . The episode with the carved manikin formed the climax and the conclusion of my childhood. It lasted about a year. Thereafter I completely forgot the whole affair until I was thirty-five. Then this fragment of memory rose up again from the mists of childhood with pristine clarity. While I was engaged on the preliminary studies for my book *Wandlungen und Symbole der Libido,* I read about the cache of soul-stones near Arlesheim, and the Australian *churingas.* I suddenly discovered that I had a quite definite image of such a stone, though I had never seen any reproductions. It was oblong, blackish, and painted into an upper and lower half. This image was joined by that of the pencil box and the manikin. The manikin was a little cloaked god of the ancient world, a Telesphoros such as stands on the monuments of Asklepios and reads to him from a scroll. Along with this recollection there came to me, for the first time, the conviction that there are archaic psychic components which have entered the individual psyche without any direct line of tradition.* (pp. 22-23)

Later Jung (1961) came to understand the little manikin as

. . . a *kabir,* wrapped in his little cloak, hidden in the *kista,* and provided with a supply of life-force, the oblong black stone. But these are connections which became clear to me only much later in my life. When I was a child I performed the ritual just as I have seen it done by the natives of Africa; they act first and do not know what they are doing. Only long afterward do they reflect on what they have done.* (p. 23)

In these examples we can recognize the distinction between play per se and something else which can only be called creative imagination, or in Jung's technical term for its function in the individuation process, active imagination. Something else of great significance is also apparent in these examples. As we have seen, the child, without questions and without doubt, simply proceeds to carry out such play as it occurs to him. We can see that there is a collaboration between the unconscious fantasy images and the child's ego consciousness. But it is also clear that the lead in the process is taken by the unconscious images. This distinction as to the relationship of the unconscious fantasy and ego consciousness in active imagination was something that Jung pondered over for many years. His most considered opinion on the process as it takes place in adults is expressed as follows (Jung, 1972):

. . . [A] dark impulse is the ultimate arbiter of the pattern, an unconscious *a priori* precipitates itself into plastic form, and one has no inkling that another person's consciousness is being guided by these same principles at the very point where one feels utterly ex-

---

*For a discussion of the Telesphoros figure, the kabir and the kista, see Daniel C. Noel, "Veiled Kabir: C. G. Jung's Phallic Self-Image," *Spring 1974,* p. 238.

posed to the boundless subjective vagaries of chance. Over the whole procedure there seems to reign a dim foreknowledge not only of the pattern but of its meaning. Image and meaning are identical; and as the first takes shape, so the latter becomes clear. Actually, the pattern needs no interpretation: it portrays its own meaning. There are cases where I can let interpretation go as a therapeutic requirement. (par. 402)

For the child, then, we can say that symbolic play is a direct analogue to active imagination and that as a spontaneous activity, it serves the purposes of individuation in childhood. That is to say, the psychological development of the child, which is of course under the prime goal of "growing up," is accomplished essentially through the normal functioning of play and the imagination. From this perspective we can say that play is an ordering principle in life. It is of ancient, prehuman origin, and as such belongs to the primordial inheritance of the psyche which includes the emotions and the archetypal regulatory functions of the psyche.

# III
# From Play to Sandplay

In its immediate origins as a vehicle of psychotherapy and Jungian analysis, sandplay can be traced on the one hand to a playful father and his two young sons who played by the hour with miniature figures, blocks, and various ordinary materials to create exciting games on the floor of their home. The noted author H. G. Wells was the playful parent, and eventually he wrote his book *Floor Games* describing the delights of these games for the edification of other parents, and as a stimulus to the manufacture of more adequate toys for children.

But Wells had a more comprehensive agenda consistent with his general aims of goading humanity into more imaginative goals for future living (Wells, 1911/1975): "Upon such a floor may be made an infinitude of imaginative games, not only keeping boys and girls happy for days together, but building up a framework of spacious and inspiring ideas in them for after life. The men of tomorrow will gain new strength from nursery floors" (p. 10). And railing aginst the inadequacies of toy manufacturers:

> We see rich people, rich people out of motor cars, rich people beyond the dreams of avarice, going into toyshops and buying these skimpy, sickly, ridiculous pseudo-boxes of bricklets, because they do not know what to ask for, and the toyshops are just the merciless mercenary enemies of youth and happiness—so far, that is, as bricks are concerned. Their unfortunate under-parented offspring mess about with these gifts, and don't make very much of them, and put them away; and you see their consequences in after life in the weakly-conceived villas and silly suburbs that people have built all round big cities. (pp. 20-21)

And when Wells talks of the toys we hear the same dissatisfactions that every sandplay therapist still experiences today:

> . . . [W]e want civilians very badly. We found a box of German civilians once in a shop, the right size but rather heavy, and running to nearly five cents apiece (which is too dear), gentlemen in tweed suits carrying bags, a top-hatted gentleman, ladies in gray and white, two children, and a dog, and so on, but we have never been able to find any more. They do not seem to be made at all—will toy manufacturers please note? I write now as if I were Consul-General in Toyland, noting new opportunities for trade. Consequent upon this dearth, our little world suffers from an exaggerated curse of militarism, and even the grocer wears epaulettes. . . . I wish, indeed, that we could buy boxes of tradesmen: a blue butcher, a white baker with a loaf of standard bread, a merchant or so; boxes of servants, boxes of street traffic, smart sets, and so forth. We could do with a judge and lawyers, or a box of vestrymen. (pp. 25-27)

In conclusion he modestly asserts: ". . . I set out merely to tell of the ordinary joys of playing with the floor, and to gird improvingly and usefully at toymakers. So much, I think, I have done. If one parent or one uncle buys the wiselier for me, I shall not altogether have lived in vain" (p. 94).

It is evident from the foregoing that Wells, in his twofold endorsement of the parental pleasures of imaginative play with one's children, and the beneficial influences of such play on future citizens and their creations, had a well formed idea of the role of play in childhood. Moreover, in his own enthusiasm for the games that he played with his sons it is evident that the spirit of play was alive and well in him. In a very real sense then his unique little book owes its origins to the lively presence of the "eternal child."

Read by Margaret Lowenfeld when she was young, Wells's book left a lasting impression, and when many years later she turned from pediatrics to establish her Institute of Child Psychology in London, it occurred to her to provide such materials for the children. Then, in that natural and spontaneous way which reveals the quality of genius, she had some shallow trays made in which sand and water were easily available. The children took it from there, for they found ready at hand the basic tools of their everyday creative life. Lowenfeld notes that the children in her clinic came to call the box of toys the "world," and soon they spontaneously combined the toys and the sandtrays. Thus it may be said in all seriousness that children have been responsible for creation of the technique. However, what was required for it to become a vehicle of psychotherapy was the lively presence of the "eternal child" in two creative adults, H. G. Wells and Margaret Lowenfeld.

From another perspective, however, it might appear that children did not so much create the world technique, as Margaret Lowenfeld has suggested, as re-initiate adults into their mode of symbolic play. In this interpretation we would be starting from our observation that children, quite on their own, have always and everywhere played in this way and with the very same materials, mother earth and the toys of Dionysus. And this is so simply because of the nature of childhood and the nature of play which, as the dynamic aspect of fantasy, continually serves to equilibrate the child's inner world of mythological apperception with the outer world of everyday life.

The succeeding stage in the sandplay migration brings us to Dora Kalff, whose adaptation of the world technique as Sandspiel was the catalyst for its widespread use among psychotherapists and analysts of Jungian persuasion. Through her personal enthusiasm and unstinting efforts to introduce others to sandplay, Kalff has singlehandedly generated a community of sandplay therapists in the United States and elsewhere. There are probably many individual reasons why sandplay appeals to Jungian analysts, but a common denominator is certainly to be found in the fact that sandplay provides a natural mirror of C. G. Jung's theories. In particular, Dora Kalff relates how in her experience she has found analogues to Jung's process of individuation in her work with children and adolescents (Kalff, 1971, p. 12). It is no accident of course that sandplay should be a natural vehicle for the confirmation of Jung's theories since, as we shall see, Jung himself had prefigured sandplay.

# IV
# Play and
# Active Imagination

Second in importance perhaps only to his conceptualization of the collective unconscious was C. G. Jung's discovery of play as the dynamic aspect of fantasy, providing the function of equilibration between consciousness and unconsciousness. As he first formulated it in 1921 in *Psychological Types* (Jung, 1971), Jung praises the principle of fantasy:

> . . . We know that every good idea and all creative work are the offspring of the imagination, and have their source in what one is pleased to call infantile fantasy. Not the artist alone, but every creative individual whatsoever owes all that is greatest in his life to fantasy. The dynamic principle of fantasy is *play*, a characteristic also of the child, and as such it appears inconsistent with the prin-

ciple of serious work. But without this playing with fantasy no creative work has ever yet come to birth. The debt we owe to the play of imagination is incalculable. (par. 93)

This praise of fantasy and play can be understood fully only in the light of Jung's memoirs (Jung, 1961), in which for the first time he revealed publicly the personal source of his conviction as to the merits of fantasy and play. There he describes in moving terms the spiritual malaise which followed upon his "parting of the ways with Freud." The state of disorientation in which he found himself led him to a recognition of the problem that his studies of mythology had posed for him: the disturbing realization that he lacked any myth that he could live by (p. 170). He sought relief through analysis of his dreams and through a reexamination of his entire life, with emphasis on his early memories and childhood, but to no avail. At last with no conscious solution at hand he decided to do whatever might be suggested to him by the unconscious:

> The first thing that came to the surface was a childhood memory from perhaps my tenth or eleventh year. At that time I had a spell of playing passionately with building blocks. I distinctly recalled how I had built little houses and castles, using bottles to form the sides of gates and vaults. Somewhat later I had used ordinary stones, with mud for mortar. . . . To my astonishment, this memory was accompanied by a good deal of emotion. . . . The small boy is still around and possesses a creative life which I lack. (pp. 173–4)

Jung then decided that the only solution to his malaise was to attempt to recover the creative life which he had possessed as a boy and which his memory suggested was still alive. But how to return to that boy, to become again a child? His solution was to do what that boy had done, to play, and moreover to play exactly what he remembered that boy to have played, a game of "building houses, castles, a whole village." So he played by the side of the lake near his home for some time, until he came to the altar of his church, which gave him pause. The church was

> . . . a square building with a hexagonal drum on top of it, and a dome. A church also requires an altar, but I hesitated to build that.

Preoccupied with the question of how I could approach this task, I was walking along the lake as usual one day, picking stones out of the gravel on the shore. Suddenly I caught sight of a red stone, a four-sided pyramid about an inch and a half high. It was a fragment of stone which had been polished into this shape by the action of the water—a pure product of chance. I knew at once: this was the altar! I placed it in the middle under the dome, and as I did so, I recalled the underground phallus of my childhood dream. This connection gave me a feeling of satisfaction. (p. 174)

How significant this memory was for Jung can be understood only in reference to the experiences of his early childhood which are related in the first chapter of his memoirs. There one learns that perhaps the most important experience of his childhood was this dream of the "chthonian God" (the underground phallus), to which in retrospect he attributed the first stirrings of his intellectual life. Buoyed up by the satisfaction of recalling the dream, Jung went on with his building game every day, noon and evening. In the course of this play he began to acquire a new understanding of what his goal was (1961):

My thoughts clarified, and I was able to grasp the fantasies whose presence in myself I dimly felt.

Naturally, I thought about the significance of what I was doing and asked myself, "Now really, what are you about? You are building a small town, and doing it as if it were a rite." I had no answer to my question, only the inner certainty that I was on the way to discovering my own myth. For the building game was only a beginning. It released a stream of fantasies which later I carefully wrote down.

This sort of thing has been consistent with me, and at any time in my later life when I came up against a blank wall, I painted a picture or hewed stone. Each such experience proved to be a *rite d'entrée* for the ideas and works that followed hard upon it. (pp. 174-5)

What Jung had discovered in his "building game" was that play did not necessarily lead down the slope of memory to childishness, but rather led directly to the unfinished business of childhood, represented in his early dream of the underground phallus. This connected him once again with the theme that had preoccupied him throughout his childhood. Following that discovery, as he says, he found that his continued playing unleashed a flood of fantasies which he religiously wrote down, sometimes drew and painted, and always sought to understand.

But there were further discoveries to be made in this process which Jung had set in motion. First of all he began to take a more "active" conscious attitude toward the fantasies. And he began a concerted effort to introvert libido, that is to focus attention and interest on the inner processes and the fantasies which appeared. In one of these efforts he imagined that he was digging a hole in the ground, a shaft which he could follow down into the earth, and this led to a new level of unconscious fantasies. Finally he began to engage in dialogue with the "personalities" encountered, and this brought him to the essence of his technique of active imagination.

The significance of this period in Jung's life cannot be over-emphasized. As he states (1961):

> It has taken me virtually forty-five years to distill within the vessel of my scientific work the things I experienced and wrote down at that time. As a young man my goal had been to accomplish something in my science. But then, I hit upon this stream of lava, and the heat of its fires reshaped my life. That was the primal stuff which compelled me to work upon it, and my works are a more or less successful endeavor to incorporate this incandescent matter into the contemporary picture of the world.
>
> The years when I was pursuing my inner images were the most important in my life—in them everything essential was decided. It all began then; the later details are only supplements and clarifications of the material that burst forth from the unconscious, and at first swamped me. It was the *prima materia* for a lifetime's work. (p. 199)

The first fruits of these labors are to be found in *Psychological Types* (1921/1971), where Jung elaborated his theories of fantasy and imagination in relation to the individuation process. He first presents his view that personality tends almost inevitably to develop in a one-sided way. Certain functions of the psyche are favored and become more highly developed than others. Here he is referring to the attitudes of introversion and extraversion, and to the four ego functions: thinking, feeling, sensation, and intuition. The less developed functions remain largely unconscious and in a relatively primitive, undeveloped state which is detrimental to individuality and wholeness. It is necessary to retrieve the undeveloped functions from the unconscious so that they may be strengthened and developed in the light of ego-consciousness. For this a bridge to the unconscious is needed, and it is here that fantasy and the imagination come in.

For Jung, fantasy is the specific and autonomous activity of the psyche, and like every other vital process of the organism it is perpetually creative. Moreover, fantasy is in a sense the mother of all functions; hence fantasy is as much thinking as feeling, and as much sensation as intuition (Jung, 1971):

> There is no psychic function that, through fantasy, is not inextricably bound up with the other psychic functions . . . it is the mother of all possibilities, where, like all psychological opposites, the inner and outer worlds are joined together in living union. Fantasy it was and ever is which fashions the bridge between the irreconcilable claims of subject and object, introversion and extraversion. In fantasy alone both mechanisms are united. (par. 78)

However, Jung is careful to distinguish active from passive fantasy. For it is active fantasy in which ego-consciousness participates with the fantasy images evoked from the unconscious and this is the process that Jung later came to call active imagination. It can take place in many forms: drawing, painting, dramatic dialogues, and so on, including, of course, sandplay.

The ultimate discovery which Jung made in his long period of self-exploration was that, first through his "building game" and then through his active engagement with the constellated fantasies, he had set in motion an ongoing process of psychological development. And his conclusion from his own experience and his observations of his patients was that this process had aim and purpose (Jung, 1966):

It is in the first place a purely natural process, which may in some cases pursue its course without the knowledge or assistance of the individual, and can sometimes forcibly accomplish itself in the face of opposition. The meaning and purpose of the process is the realization, in all its aspects, of the personality originally hidden away in the embryonic germ-plasm; the production and unfolding of the original, potential wholeness. The symbols used by the unconscious to this end are the same as those which mankind has always used to express wholeness, completeness, and perfection: symbols, as a rule, of the quaternity and the circle. For these reasons I have termed this the *individuation process.* (par. 186)

# V
# Summary and Conclusions

In our brief survey we have traced sandplay to its roots in the symbolic play of childhood. And we have seen that the child's symbolic play appears to serve the process of individuation in childhood, seemingly as an analogue to adult active imagination. As for the play impulse, its roots are to be found in the ancient inherited psyche which includes the emotions and the archetypal regulatory functions. Play appears to have evolved to fill an ontogenetic gap left by the "bursting of programmed instinct" that heralded emergence of the mammalian species. Its fundamental purpose seems to be the equilibration of states of *being* and *becoming,* primarily during the developmental stages of immaturity. In humans, through its dual functions of bridging between ego-consciousness and the unconscious and making possible creative imagination, it reveals an aspect of the "eternal child" and ultimately an expression of the self. Here we can identify the meaning of Schiller's famous pronouncement on the significance of play. Jung (1975) writes: "The creative activity of imagination frees man from his bondage to the 'nothing but' and raises him to the status of one who plays. As Schiller says, man is completely human only when he is at play" (par. 98).

As one of the several techniques of active imagination, sandplay has the particular merits of, first, requiring no special skills or talents for the use of the materials, and second, and most important, providing a direct link to the play world of childhood. Thus for the child in therapy, sandplay is a purely natural mode of expression, for it is nothing more nor less than the symbolic play which the child ordinarily engages in at every opportunity, and through which, in the normal course of growing up, the two realms of being, the inner world of archetypal apperception and the outer world of everyday reality, are mediated. But, of course, the child who is brought for treatment suffers from emotionally charged conflicts which have blocked normal development and inhibited normal symbolic play. A special milieu is required to revive spontaneous play and to free creative imagination. This is accomplished through the therapist's comforting presence and wholehearted acceptance. Together these create the "free and sheltered space" (Kalff, 1971, p. 18) within which the child feels safe enough to play out his conflicts in the sandtray, thus reestablishing the normal relationship between developing ego-consciousness and the unconscious.

For adults in Jungian analysis, sandplay may provide that *rite d'entrée* which Jung described. By playing again like a child, with all the seriousness of a child at play, the adult revives lost memories, releases unconscious fantasies, and in the course of time, constellates the images of reconciliation and wholeness of the individuation process. The effectiveness of the technique for the adult lies in what Jung, with his profound insight, discovered: that the fantasy world of childhood is not a world to be transcended; on the contrary (Jung, 1971), "the images are not lost, but come again in ripe manhood and should be fulfilled" (par. 436). In conclusion, then, we are brought to the realization that the child as archetype is, as Jung says (1968a), "both beginning and end, an initial and a terminal creature" (par. 299). The child archetype expresses psychic wholeness (Jung, 1968a):

> The "child" is all that is abandoned and exposed and at the same time divinely powerful; the insignificant, dubious beginning, and the triumphal end. The "eternal child" in man is an indescribable experience, an incongruity, a handicap, and a divine prerogative; an imponderable that determines the ultimate worth or worthlessness of a personality. (par. 300)

# The Developmental Psychology
# of Sandplay

CHARLES T. STEWART

One of the dilemmas which confronts the child therapist is what to do about play. This is one of those problems that will not go away, for given a modicum of freedom all children, except the most severely disturbed, persist in devoting some of their therapy time to play, even in the most barren clinical settings. My first confrontation with this dilemma lasted ten years. It began in 1956, the year I began two years of training in child psychiatry; it continued through eight years of practice in a community child guidance clinic; and it ended in 1966, the year I first met Dora Kalff and entered full-time private practice. During this decade the perplexity and conflict over play which I and my fellow therapists experienced took various forms. There was always the basic question about the legitimacy of a lengthy, costly, therapeutic procedure which was mostly, after all, "nothing but" play. In what we would now call the ecological domain, the dilemma was reflected in small, ill-equipped playrooms which often stood empty and unused. Then there were the spirited but inconclusive debates over the nature and function of play. To add further complication, each theory generated its own answers to the urgent practical questions we posed. Should we interpret his play to the child at all? If so, should it be only within the metaphor? Should play be encouraged, discouraged as a defense, or left to the spontaneous impulse of the child? Were there toys and games which should be in every play-

room? Were there toys and games which should not be in any
playroom? For the most part our answers lacked conviction and
cohesion.

In retrospect I can see that the events which transformed my attitude to play and ended my dilemma actually began in the fall of
1964, when I first learned (from Louis H. Stewart) of Margaret
Lowenfeld's world technique and Frau Kalff's adaptation of it. I
began to consider how this method could be applied to a community setting. In June, 1965 I wrote to Frau Kalff, who replied without delay that she would be pleased to introduce her technique to
our clinic when she was in San Francisco the following February.
She also sent a translation of "Archetypus als heilender Faktor"
(Kalff, 1964) containing a description of her method, and said that
a book on her therapy would be published in the spring. The next
step in the transformative process was my decision that fall to leave
community work the following June and enter full-time private
practice—a decision that only intensified the play dilemma by
translating it into the practical choice of how to furnish my personal consulting room.

Between Frau Kalff's letter and her visit to the Bay Area we had
agreed that during her visit she would address one of our monthly
community mental health meetings. Thus, on February 24, 1966, it
was my privilege first to introduce Frau Kalff to an overflow audience and next to join that audience in its gasps of astonishment and
delight when her first slides were projected to reveal those magical
shelves in her office in Zurich, crowded with an endless profusion
of animated toy figures. By the end of her lecture the play dilemma, for me, was over. I knew at once that here was being expressed, in theory and in practice, an attitude toward play that was
worthy of one's deepest commitment. I decided to introduce
sandplay into my practice, and the Lowenfeld apparatus was in
place when I began it that July.

The next decade, 1966-1976, was for me a time for the clinical
application of sandplay, for the systematic collection of data in the
form of photographic slides of completed trays (I also kept records
of parallel or sequential use of other expressive forms—dreams,
drawings, modelings, paintings, games, etc.), and for a more pur-

poseful reading of the literature. This reading revealed that a quiet revolution in play theory was in progress, which was slowly eroding the "nothing but" attitude toward play (Sutton-Smith, 1976). My first articulation of these experiences began in 1978 in collaboration with Louis Stewart, when we offered a series of courses on sand worlds through U.C. Extension in Berkeley. Two collaborative papers followed the next year, one presented (Stewart and Stewart, Note 6) and one unpublished (Stewart and Stewart, Note 7). The latter deals with the growth stages of ego-identity in the affective transformations in play and active imagination, and this article is a direct extension of that paper.

The purpose of this study is to introduce a method for the developmental analysis of sandplay configurations in order to facilitate their use as clinical and research materials. Our review of the literature can be brief since there are only two previous works concerned specifically with this topic. It was Dora Kalff (1965, 1971) who first directed our attention to the applicability of Neumann's stages of psychological growth to the analysis of sandplay constructions. When she viewed the configurations made by her patients in the light of Neumann's stages of ego development, the results coincided with her own observations. The other relevant study is the research of Ruth Bowyer, which appears as Chapter 4, "The Search for Developmental Norms," in her book *The Lowenfeld World Technique* (1970), where she reports the results of her analyses of worlds made by 26 "normal" and 24 "clinical" children, ages 2 through 16 years.* Bowyer selected Kurt Lewin's topological psychology as the basis for the analysis of the three-dimensional Lowenfeld worlds. More specifically, Bowyer used Lewin's developmental parameters of (1) increase in life space, (2) increase in realism, and (3) increase in differentiation-integration as the respective analytic categories of (a) use of the tray, (b) fantasy-reality dimension, and (c) the use of sand and part-whole relation-

---

*A number of informative studies of symbolic or world play have been excluded from this review because their methods involve some radical alteration of the basic apparatus, such as using a table and eliminating the sand, etc., but the references to these researches appear in Bowyer's bibliographies.

ships. When she applied her method to the worlds made by the 26 normal children, she distinguished four chronological stages, 2 to 4, 5 to 7, 8 to 10, and 11+ years, with characteristic developmental differences in the use of the tray, the use of sand, etc. Her specific results will be presented in more detail in the application section of this paper.

In referring to the method introduced here as analytic, I am following the distinction between interpretation and analysis drawn by Richard Jones (1962) in his presentation of a method for the epigenetic analysis of the manifest content of dreams. He concludes his discussion of this issue as follows:

> In order to assure continued clarity on these points: the therapeutically effective interpretation of a dream is almost always an existential-phenomenological interpretation, precisely because of its uniqueness; the wishfulfillment and epigenetic interpretations of a dream are almost never therapeutically effective, precisely because of their regularity. I propose that we reserve the term interpretation for the art, and the term analysis for the science. None of this is to say, of course, that the scientist may not profit from his artistic interests, nor the artist from his scientific interests. (p. 49)

The method presented here is intended for the analysis of sandtrays in, for example, the clinical or research context. When such analysis occurs to the therapist during a clinical interview, it may provide input for the adoption of a therapeutic stance, or for the formulation of an interpretive comment which he then might offer to the patient.

After describing the method, I shall illustrate its application to a series of sandtrays made by children under 12. I hope this will provide a step toward the establishment of sandplay norms. Extension of the method to sandtrays made at other stages of the life cycle is reserved for a future work.

# Method

The method introduced here consists of three elements: (1) the definition of a sandplay text; (2) a chronological, sequential stage representation of psychic development; and (3) a developmental hierarchy of games as an explanatory model.

### DEFINITION OF A SANDPLAY TEXT

Let me first say a word about the process of sandplay as opposed to the completed sandtray. Just how a sand world is constructed, quickly or slowly, in a complex way or simply, ought to be part of the data available for clinical or research purposes—even though this information may not tell us anything about what the sand world means to the patient who made it. Such data would complement, not replace, the information sought from photographing completed trays. Since at present, however, no one has devised a simple, practical method for recording the details of the construction process, analysis has to be confined to the finished product.

But one fact that has already emerged from the continued clinical observation of sandplay, both as process and completed configuration, is that the content of the worlds is related to what Eric Klinger (1971) has defined, in respect to fantasy, as the individual's "current concerns": "Both play and fantasy reflect current focal concerns of the individual—unresolved current problems, unfinished tasks, role conflicts, and prominent affective responses, as well as the challenges of identity and commitment posed by the individual's social relationships" (p. 49). This fact directs us to ensure that our analysis of worlds is always in *context,* and it follows from this perspective that a sandtray is a play *text.*

With the terms text and context we have moved into a conceptual domain which methodologically connects sociolinguistic language development studies (e.g., Halliday, 1975) and studies of the development of ludic action.* In two complementary papers Brian

---

*The use of the word ludic follows that of Sutton-Smith (1971c): "The term *ludic* as used here is derived from the Latin term for play after Huizinga (1949). Play and games will be referred to jointly as ludic behavior systems, by which is implied behavioral, verbal or nonverbal, or symbolic events of a systemic character. There are patterns to these behaviors just as there are to any others . . ." (p. 75).

Sutton-Smith (1977a, 1977b) has reviewed the principles involved and concluded that either type of one-sided analysis, context without text or text without context, must be considered methodologically unsound. Two extracts from the former article will clarify this point.

> The sociolinguistic approach . . . implies that in looking for the origins of the structure of ludic action, one should look first to the socio-communicational context in which these actions first took place. To understand play, that is, one should begin with the study of mother-infant play. One should *not* begin with the study of the solitary play of the individual infant. . . . The latter behaviors are largely derived from the earlier and higher level communicational play of mother and infant. One could learn about play in the solitary context only what Chomsky has learned about language in the grammatical context. That is, one could learn something of the embedded constitutive rules that govern play but would not understand either their origin or their appropriate regulative application. . . . (p. 239)

> Enough illustrations have been given to indicate the value of the present sociolinguistic approach to a theory of ludic action. It is hardly possible to talk about the dramatic action of games without prior references to these communicational systems and subsystems within which that dramatic action takes place, although we have ourselves tried to do just that. . . . Enough evidence has been given also to modify the view that one can take a communicational (sometimes called a contextual) approach to folk structure or a simply dramatic (sometimes called textual) approach. While there are extremes of both, what we see throughout development is a variety of communicational frames linked to a variety of dramatic structures at various developmental levels. (p. 248)

Our consideration of these principles was one of the factors which led us to include a definition of a sandplay text as a component of our method.

Another factor was our awareness that among the important contemporary contributions to the development of play theory has been the discrimination of play from other significant behaviors, such as exploration, experimentation, curiosity, imitation, etc. (Hutt, 1966; Sutton-Smith, 1971a). This indicates that our definition must be formulated so as to exclude the most critical area of non-play, exploration, from consideration for analysis. For example, a child may alter the initial sandtray pattern by patting or poking areas of the dry and the wet sand to compare their textures. Or he may push sand aside to obtain a better view of the blue bottom of the tray. Occasionally a child will ripple the surface of the sand, not in play, but while running his hands along the inner surface of the sides of the tray to explore the smoothness of the wood. Each of these behaviors is an example of curiosity-exploration and any alteration in a sandtray resulting from these or like actions will not be considered amenable to analysis by the method introduced here.

We can begin our discussion of what is included in the definition by citing a relevant passage from "Sandplay Therapy: Jungian Technique" (Stewart, 1977):

> On the basis of this brief survey of the relevant theory, we see that sandplay takes its place as one of the several techniques of active imagination. . . . For the child in therapy, sandplay is a purely natural mode of expression. It is, after all, nothing more or less than the symbolic play in which the child ordinarily engages at every opportunity. . . . (p. 11)

This characterization of sand world constructions as symbolic play meets our needs for inclusiveness with one possible exception: it may exclude sand worlds made by infants (or rather, the presentation of stages of infant development in worlds made at later stages of growth). Let me clarify this. Piaget has described cognitive development in infancy (from birth to about 18 months) as sensori-motor, a designation intended to convey his view of its practical, non-representative nature. In his major work on play (1962), he has defined play in infancy as practice play, to differentiate it from symbolic or representative play, which he considers to develop during the second year with the beginning of pretense. Thus if we wish to make the presentation of infant developmental stages in sand worlds available for analysis, and we do; the definition of a sandplay text must include both practice and symbolic play. (The reasons for this emphasis on infancy will become evident when we discuss stages of development and in the first section on application below.)

We are now at the point where we can define a sandplay construction:

*A sandplay text is any alteration in a sandtray constituted by a play act or by play actions.*

The generality of this definition will insure the applicability of our method to all stages of the life cycle.

### STAGES OF PSYCHIC DEVELO MENT

Parents, educators, juvenile court judges, etc., frequently ask the child specialist to determine if a given child is "normal" or not. When this is a genuine question (not a pseudo-question which actually seeks leverage in an argument or support for an intended action), my experience is that one's attempts to answer undergo a progression of their own; initially one replies in terms of psychopathology; at the next level one defines "normality" as a matter of opinion, and tends to interpret the question as a defense (which it often is). However, the child specialist who has assimilated Jung's precept that a neurosis is an unsuccessful adaptation will finally be motivated to seek a more reflective answer to the question of normality. I was attempting to establish for myself a conception of normal development when my interest also turned to devising a method for the developmental study of sandplay, and it became apparent that the optimal context for such analysis, and therefore a necessary component of my method, was a comprehensive theory of development.

My review revealed three theories of development which were preeminently adequate, those of Neumann (1962, 1973), Erikson (1963), and Piaget (1969). Of these, Neumann's appeared to be the most comprehensive. This statement may require elaboration. Let me begin with a quotation from Piaget (1970a).

> The fundamental hypothesis of genetic epistemology is that there is a parallelism between the progress made in the logical and rational organization of knowledge and the corresponding formative

psychological processes. Well, now, if that is our hypothesis, what will be our field of study? Of course the most fruitful, most obvious field of study would be reconstituting human history—the history of human thinking in prehistoric man. Unfortunately, we are not very well informed about the psychology of Neanderthal man or about the psychology of *Homo siniensis* of Teilhard de Chardin. Since this field of biogenesis is not available to us, we shall do as biologists do and turn to ontogenesis. Nothing could be more accessible to study than the ontogenesis of these notions. There are children all around us. (p. 13)

From Neumann's perspective as *cultural* psychologist, as well as depth psychologist, he could first envision the possibility of reconstructing the phylogenesis of ego-consciousness, using the phenomenology of myth, and then proceed to demonstrate it in *The Origins and History of Consciousness* (1962). Then in *The Child* (1973) he could present the ontogenetic parallel to this phylogenetic development. A reading of these works reveals that Neumann has fully assimilated Piaget's cognitive system and that Erikson would agree with most of his criticisms of traditional Freudian developmental theory.

It is true, however, that Neumann's synthesis is often implicit rather than explicit, so that viewing the three theories in conjunction still offers certain advantages. Consequently I decided to try to synthesize the three systems, an attempt which, surprisingly, had not previously been made. There was already an illuminating, useful synthesis and extension, from a dynamic, educational perspective, of the theories of Piaget and Erikson (Jones, 1968). And methodological support for my project appeared in a paper by Reese and Overton (1970) establishing that these three systems were all in the same theoretical family and therefore amenable to integration.

I discovered that Piaget and Erikson (along with a group of distinguished colleagues including Margaret Mead, Konrad Lorenz, John Bowlby, and Ludwig von Bertalanffy) had discussed the integration of theories of development at an International Conference on Child Development. The report is given by Tanner and Inhelder (1960). First Piaget:

In order to describe development "synthetically" and, above all, to make some progress in the explanation of these general mechanisms, it is essential to have a common language. Indeed, without a common language we shall never succeed in analysing the actual interactions between the factors and will always return, despite ourselves, to a description by juxtaposition (or accumulation) of influences. . . . As soon as we adopt this broader viewpoint, as imposed on us by the search for a common language, we perceive that there exists a fourth factor, more general than the three classic factors of innateness, physical experience and social environment, and obeying its own special laws of probability and the minimum: this is the factor of *equilibrium* which is found associated with each of the three preceding ones, but which governs particularly their interactions and which, moreover, reveals itself frequently in an independent manner. . . . In the field of affective development it would be particularly interesting to translate social and dynamic psychoanalysis, as understood by Bowlby and Erikson, into the language of equilibrium. (pp. 5-8)

Next Erikson:

When Barbel Inhelder is testing a child, that child is supposed, for example, to match cards depicting two containers of water. But he may for a moment become more interested in seeing the water run out of the upper container into the lower container than in concentrating on the cognitive problem. In other words anyone motivated to concentrate on the cognitive has to suppress the mere enjoyment of making the thing function and the playful wish to match things aesthetically. Professor Piaget told us yesterday something about the equilibrium of the cognitive function. But as this is being established there must be some more general tendency in the child which permits him to concentrate on that which will lead to a cognitive equilibrium and to exclude other aspects of the mind which are seeking *their* kind of equilibrium: the psychosexual, the psychosocial, etc. This equilibrator behind all equilibrated functions is, I think, what we call the ego in psychoanalysis. (p. 146)

Neumann as well was mindful of the need for a common language and conceived of *centroversion* and *automorphism* as the two psychic functions which insure the optimal self-regulative interaction between the various factors contributing to psychic development.

On the following page is an epigenetic chart (Figure 1) of the proposed synthesis.

With these three contributions toward a constructive view of development in mind, and since our method is directed to the analysis of ludic configurations, the following discussion will focus on the possible synthetic function of play. That is, when we formulate our general descriptions of the periods under consideration, we shall pay special attention to the stages in the development of play, while anticipating, of course, that there will be a close correlation between the archetypal-ego, psychosocial, cognitive, and ludic structures in each period of development.

The four stages of development to be considered in this paradigmatic study are:

Infancy (Inf II): 7-10 to 12-24 months
Early Childhood I (EC I): 1-2 to 3-4 years
Early Childhood II (EC II): 3-4 to 6-7 years
Middle Childhood (MC): 6-7 to 11-12 years

Their characteristics are described in detail in the section on application.

Our view of the relationship between genesis and structure derives primarily from Piaget (1968), whose two theses are: (1) genesis emanates from a structure and culminates in another structure, and (2) conversely, every structure has a genesis. For example, the passage from concrete cognitive operations at 6 or 7 years to formal cognitive operations at 11 or 12 years is a genesis based on the fullest possible exploration of concrete operations, which in the process are integrated into the new cognitive form. Likewise, the transition from pretend play at 1 to 2 years to imaginative play at 3 to 4 years occurs through the generalization of the world of make-believe, which in the process is transformed and interiorized as fantasy play.

FIGURE I

| | INFANCY | EARLY CHILDHOOD I | EARLY CHILDHOOD II, PLAY AGE | MIDDLE CHILDHOOD, SCHOOL AGE |
|---|---|---|---|---|
| *Age (years)* | Birth to 1-2 | 1-2 to 3-4 | 3-4 to 6-7 | 6-7 to 11-12 |
| NEUMANN | | | | |
| *Archetypal Stage* | Uroboros (Infancy I) Great Mother (Infancy II) | Separation of World Parents, Birth of Hero | Transition from Matriarchy to Patriarchy, Slaying of the Dragon | Great Father |
| *Ego Stage* | Phallic-chthonian | Magic-phallic | Magic-warlike | Solar-warlike |
| ERIKSON | | | | |
| *Nuclear Crisis* | Trust v. Mistrust | Autonomy v. Shame-Doubt | Initiative v. Guilt | Industry v. Inferiority |
| *Radius of Relations* | Maternal Person | Parental Persons | Basic Family | Neighborhood, School |
| PIAGET | | | | |
| *Cognitive Stage* | Sensori-motor/ Practical Intelligence I-VI | Egocentric Representative Activity I | Egocentric Representative Activity II | Concrete Operations |
| *Morality/ Rules* | | | Objective/ Ascriptive | Subjective/ Mutual |

## AN EXPLANATORY MODEL:
## A DEVELOPMENTAL HIERARCHY OF GAMES

The purpose of this explanatory model is to reflect the organization of developmental stages at the level of the sandplay substrate, and so to help objectify the analytic process. Since setting up the model is a fundamental step in constructing this analytic method, it is important to understand the factors determining the selection of games. The basic task of selection was to choose a paradigm at the proper level of symbolic complexity, with a structural pattern relevant to the substrate.

Neumann's concept of creative evolution was one determining factor (1962):

> The evolution of consciousness as a form of creative evolution is the peculiar achievement of Western man. Creative evolution of ego consciousness means that, through a continuous process stretching over thousands of years, the conscious system has absorbed more and more unconscious contents and progressively extended its frontiers. Although from antiquity right down to recent times we see a new and differently patterned canon of culture continually superseding the previous one, the West has nevertheless succeeded in achieving an historical and cultural continuity in which each canon gradually came to be integrated. The structure of modern consciousness rests on this integration, and at each period of its development the ego has to absorb essential portions of the cultural past transmitted to it by the canon of values embodied in its own culture and system of education. (Volume I, p. xviii)

It follows that our model must function at the sociocultural level.

Now we know that there are two sources of games: (1) the codification of social play, and (2) the transmission of religious and social rituals which have become ludic forms. In essence games are the cultural form of play. This basis for our choice of games has been considerably strengthened by the following two closely related factors. The first is that significant relationships exist between games and other cultural variables, such as child-rearing practices, social order, etc. (Caillois, 1961; Roberts and Sutton-Smith, 1962). The second is the connection suggested between games and the primary affects (the archetypes), as presented in the following observation (Stewart and Stewart, Note 6):

> The popularity of any game is dependent upon its meeting particular social and cultural needs which reflect the mythical origins and structure of the society. This accounts for the preference for types of games in any specific society and the myriad local variations on

typical games. However the universal aspects of games derive from the fundamental invariants of the human condition of which, we suggest, the affects are a baseline determinant. (p. 11)

A methodological principle directing our selection of games as model is the preference for using one ludic pattern, games, as the structural descriptive model for another ludic system, spontaneous play (Sutton-Smith, 1971b). This correlates at the theoretical level with our final factor: in the most comprehensive of the modern theories of play, games are noted as sharing in all of the integrative and innovative characteristics of play with the addition, because of their social nature, that games also function to transcend and transform the conflicts of interpersonal experience (Sutton-Smith, 1976).

The selection of the specific developmental sequences of games to be used is based on my own and others' empirical observations as well as on the theoretical framework provided in the conflict-enculturation theory of games formulated by Roberts and Sutton-Smith (1962). In capsule form, this theory states that the individual and psychological motivation for game playing is the presence in the player of anxieties and conflicts induced by antecedent child-training practices. The game is a symbolic statement of these conflicts, and, in the course of the buffered learning that the game provides, the player develops confidence and competence to handle the real-life situations toward which the original anxieties point. Thus in establishing their developmental psychology of games, the Sutton-Smiths (1974) based their classification on the types of conflicts or oppositions they discerned in the games.

The way we visualize the hierarchy of games through which children develop is as follows:
Games of *order and disorder* ("Ring around the Rosy") [4-5]*
Games of *approach and avoidance* [5-6]
  Chasing and escaping (tag)

---

*The numbers in brackets are the approximate chronological ages in years proposed by Roberts and Sutton-Smith (1962) for each step in the hierarchy.

Acceptance and rejection ("The Farmer in the Dell")
Domination and usurpation (Mother May I)
Attack and defense (football, chess)
Games of *success and failure* [9-13]
Accumulation and deprivation (bingo)
Correctness or mistakes (jump rope)
Scoring or being outscored (marbles)

A game then becomes an opposition between forces with an uncertain outcome and with rules controlling the character of the events. (p. 243)

We can now present, in relation to the stages of development outlined in the previous section, the hierarchy of games which we have established as the explanatory component of the method presented here. Descriptions of the specific characteristics of the games will be given in the section on application, along with the details of the stages. The games listed in parentheses are paradigmatic, that is they are the game type for the particular stage of development under consideration; many other specific games present the same or a similar structure.

Infancy II (Inf II): 7-10 to 12-24 months
Games of appearance and disappearance  (Peek-a-boo)
Early Childhood I (EC I): 1-2 to 3-4 years
Games of order and disorder  (Ring around the Rosy)
Early Childhood II (EC II): 3-4 to 6-7 years
Central-person games (tag)
Middle Childhood (MC): 6-7 to 11-12 years
Games of peer sexual differentiation  (jacks, marbles)

APPLICATION

Each demonstration analysis will consist of (1) a characterization of the game model correlative with the level of development, (2) a description of the stage of development, and (3) application of the game pattern to the sandplay text.

The sandtrays used in the following analyses appear in the report by Bowyer or were made by children in psychotherapy with the author. These children were presented with a standard Lowenfeld apparatus consisting of one tray with dry sand, another tray with wet sand, and a wide variety of miniature life figures. As previously indicated, all of the worlds discussed were made by children under 12 years of age.


## Infancy II (Inf II): 7-10 to 12-24 months
## Games of appearance and disappearance
## (Peek-a-boo)


As we will not present sandtrays made by infants (Bowyer's youngest subject was 22 months old and we have no earlier data) and do not think that they are necessary to our argument, our analysis at this level of development requires a brief introduction. Theoretically, longitudinal studies could be undertaken which would include the collection of sand worlds made by infants, and family therapists who use sandplay may already have, intentionally or inadvertently, collected such worlds. But we do not suggest that the actual collection and study of such trays is essential to our thesis. There is not only reason to attempt our analysis of the developmental stages of infancy without such data, but good reason to anticipate that it will be valid. This assertion will be less puzzling when we recall that the three developmental systems used in our method are all reconstructive, as well as constructive, and are based on the concept of hierarchical integration.

The reconstructive hypothesis, attributed to Erikson by Piaget (1970b), indicates that "we continually assimilate the past to the present with a view to adaptations in the present, just as much as our present existence depends on the past in the continuity of behaviour and representations" (p. 35).

Hierarchical integration of successive stages is defined by Flavell (1963):

> A second essential characteristic of true stages is that the structures defining earlier stages become integrated or incorporated into

those of the stages following. For instance, the stage of formal operations . . . involves cognitive activities which are performed *upon*
the concrete operations elaborated in the stage just preceding.
(p. 20)

And Richard Jones's (1962) summary of this same position in regard to his epigenetic analyses of dreams is particularly relevant to
our method for the analyses of sandtrays.

. . . [T]he dream itself in the process of its formation was engaged
in reconstructive activity, preconsciously redifferentiating and re-
integrating pre-adaptive epigenetic successes and failures in the
context of and under the problematic pressure of the phase specific
re-adaptive crises. (p. 35; original in italics)

These statements suggest that there is no theoretical impediment
to our detection of Infancy II patterns, and those of Infancy I for
that matter, in sand worlds at any of the subsequent stages of the
life cycle, whether or not we also have trays made by infants for
further empirical confirmation. They also indicate that *unless* we
can accomplish such analyses, the consideration of trays made by
subjects during the first two years, in developmental isolation so to
speak, will be of little value.

Another compelling reason for undertaking such analyses derives from the dramatic contemporary increase in our knowledge
about psychological development in infancy, which has already re-
sulted in "the first five years" being replaced by "the first three
years," which soon no doubt will be superseded by "the first
year." As there is no longer any doubt that psychological growth
in infancy is the foundation of all future personality development,
any method intended to assess levels of ego-consciousness must
include those stages occurring in infancy.

GAME MODEL

It is of interest that in fact the explanatory potential of our
method was first demonstrated at the level of Infancy II. We were
aware of the empirical evidence that the universal game from
seven to ten months is Peek-a-boo, and we knew that Peek-a-boo
was included as a test item for this age in the baby scales for infan-

cy. There was also the occasional idiosyncratic fact, such as the observation that a study of "stranger anxiety," characteristic of this same phase of growth, was nearly invalidated by the inadvertent inclusion of Peek-a-boo as one of the test items (Goulet, 1974). And we realized that Piaget's cognitive studies of the development of the object concept during this same phase of infancy (his stage IV), as well as those in his stages V and VI, were all based on hiding objects behind screens! All this was encouraging for our method, but actual projection onto the sandtrays eluded us. Then one day the spark jumped, the projection took place, and one of the most ubiquitous of all sand world behaviors suddenly took on new meaning: the behavior of burying and digging up, covering and uncovering, hiding and finding in the sand, which all who have worked with this technique know as a regular and almost incidental occurrence in most constructions, and a central theme in certain other configurations. It is this behavior that we would now designate as exemplary of Infancy II. There are times, of course, when the child will actually play Hide-and-seek in the tray, but this is another matter and need not concern us now. The nature of the object that is made to disappear and appear is also significant, but this again is not immediately germane to our discussion.

When reviewing one source of material regarding ego development in infancy, Harry Guntrip's *Schizoid Phenomena, Object-Relations, and the Self* (1968), a study of schizoid personality disorders, we were struck by the way author and patients used words and phrases that suggested the hiding-game paradigm. Here is a partial list of such usages culled from throughout the book (italics mine):

> . . . a *hidden* inner world . . . *hiding* her feelings from herself . . . one *hiding* from the world . . . I feel I'm *disappearing* . . . the threat of being *found* . . . the fantasy of being *found* . . . mother was *peeping* into . . . creeping out of the shelter of his hole to *peep* at the world.

Guntrip additionally refers us to "Communicating and Not Communicating Leading to a Study of Certain Opposites" (Chapter 17 of Winnicott, 1965), which contains the following observations. The first follows the report of a dream and an early memory by a woman patient: "Here is a picture of a child establishing a private self that is not communicating and at the same time wanting to communicate and to be found. It is a sophisticated game of hide-and-seek in which *it is a joy to be hidden but disaster to be found*" (p. 186; italics mine). The second follows an extract from an interview with a girl of seventeen: "The defence consists in a further hiding of the secret self, even in the extreme to its projection and to its endless dissemination" (p. 187).

## STAGE OF DEVELOPMENT

When we turned to an examination of Neumann's theory at this level, we found that his correlation between the stage of ego development and chronological age is most precise in infancy. Repeatedly (Neumann, 1973) he refers to infancy, the phallic-chthonian stage of ego development, as comprising two sub-phases: (1) the primal relationship (our Infancy I, birth to 7-10 months), a period of unconscious identity in which the infant's unity resides in the body-self and the mother is the relatedness-self; and (2) the "true" birth of the human infant (our Infancy II, 7-10 to 12-24 months), during which period the relatedness-self "moves" from mother to infant, uniting with the body-self to form the unified-self. This second phase of infancy is placed chronologically at the end of the first post-natal year (11-13 months). Although the entire period of infancy is matriarchal, the sub-phases are differentiated archetypally into the Uroboros and the Great Mother. Finally the culmination of this stage of development is the first configuration of the integral ego and the polarization of the world into opposites. We would speculate that the infant's experience of the "moving" may be an orderly fluctuation within the framework of the appearance-disappearance paradigm.

Our interpretation of Erikson's conceptualization of this period is that he has identified the primal relationship by the term mutuality, in particular early incorporative mutuality, and the "true" birth or weaning of the infant by the nuclear crisis of trust versus mistrust.

Without entering into a detailed discussion of the empirical evidence, we can indicate that the correlations are quite precise between Infancy I and Stages I, II, and III of Piaget's sensorimotor development and between Infancy II and his Stages IV, V, and VI of practical intelligence. Empirical intelligence is achieved in Stage IV with the first intentional coordination of ends and means behaviors, which is accompanied by the following progressions in the categories of reason and knowledge (object, space, time, and causality): the first level of object permanence; the first spatial groups, including the distinction between "in front of" and "behind"; the first temporal series, including the differentiation between "before" and "after"; and the first objectification and spatialization of causality. In this first level of object permanence and formation of spatial groups Piaget discerns what in his view are the basic characteristics of cognitive operations, conservation and reversibility. Construction continues in Stages V and VI, and by this latter phase systematic intelligence and representative categories of reason are also achieved.

The play marker at Stage VI, the end of Infancy II, is pretend or symbolic play, a phenomenon which is well known and requires no further comment. The ludic boundary at 7-10 months (between Inf I and Inf II) is less clearly defined and requires a brief discussion. Jacqueline, Piaget's eldest child, is sitting in her cot, age 9 months and 3 days (Piaget, 1962):

> Then she pulled her pillow from under her head, and having shaken it, struck it hard and struck the sides of the cot and the doll with it. As she was holding the pillow, she noticed the fringe, which she began to suck. This action, which reminded her of what she did every day before going to sleep, caused her to lie down on her side, in the position for sleep, holding a corner of the fringe and sucking her thumb. This, however, did not last for a half a minute and J. resumed her earlier activity. (p. 93)

Piaget comments:

> But there is more in such behaviors than a mere sequence of aimless combinations with no attempt at accommodation. There is what might be called a "ritualisation" of the schemas, which, no

longer in their adaptive context, are as it were imitated or "played" plastically. It is specially worth noting how J. goes through the ritual of all the actions she usually does when she is about to go to sleep (lies down, sucks her thumb, holds the fringe), merely because this schema is evoked by the circumstances. It is clear that this "ritualisation" is a preparation for symbolic games. (p. 93)

Thus we can designate the play marker at the beginning of Infancy II as gestural or figurative play, play clearly on its way to becoming symbolic.

Two of Bowyer's (1971) observations regarding the use of sand by her normal 2- to 4-year-old children are relevant in our present context. "At age 2-3+ and decreasingly until 4+ toys were poked or flung into the sand, so that they were buried or half-buried" (p. 26). She also speaks of ". . . the destructive use of sand, at ages 2-4 (pouring sand over people or things, or pushing toys into the sand, sometimes with the words 'down, down!') . . ." (p. 28).

SANDPLAY TEXT

We will conclude our presentation at this level with an extract from my clinical interview with a 6-year-old boy, which offers a sandplay text relevant to our model analysis of Infancy II. He first made two rings from red plasticine and then molded them together. Then he moved to the dry tray and placed a wild animal in it, then buried and uncovered it. With his index finger he drew a circle in the center of the tray and placed the animal inside this circle. He put three more wild animals inside the circle, then he buried and unearthed each of them separately. Then he took the four animals and covered them with sand and then uncovered them. Several more animals were introduced, each being "initiated" into the tray through what appeared to be a ritual disappearance and reappearance. Up to this point the sandplay text is considered to be at the level of Infancy II. Now confrontation and fighting erupted between the animals, only two being involved at any one time. As will be clarified in the next section, this is considered progression to the stage of Early Childhood I, which is reflected in games of order and disorder.

# Early Childhood (EC I): 1-2 to 3-4 years
# Games of order and disorder
# (Ring around the Rosy)

## GAME MODEL

One of the forms of spontaneous play in EC I, rough and tum-
ble play with its exuberance and anarchy, provides a natural link
with the games of order and disorder which we have designated as
the ludic model for this stage. On two occasions N. Blurton-Jones
(1969, 1974) has observed and described this variation of self-
motion play which, appearing as early as eighteen months, is characterized by seven movement patterns: running, chasing and flee-
ing, wrestling, "jumps," pretend hitting, laughing, and falling. In
describing the falling he reports, ". . . if there is anything soft to
land on children spend much time throwing themselves and each
other onto it" (p. 357).

The transition to Ring around the Rosy, our exemplary game
of order and disorder, is almost imperceptible, but is recorded in
the following extracts from Sutton-Smith (1977a, 1977b), which
also provide us with a formal characterization of this group of
games.

> . . . [G]ames of order and disorder are a special case, they model
> the system only to destroy it. Their ambivalence is much more
> fundamental. They are both the most fundamental form of games
> (establishing for the young the roots of cooperation) and the most
> radical (upsetting the orders of motor, conventional impulse and
> social hierarchical control). (p. 227[b])

> Everyone acts at the same time either diffusely or more or less in
> parallel, and the outcome may occur to one or all. The outcome is
> usually a motor collapse.
> The most obvious example in European culture is Ring a Ring a
> Roses, where all proceed in an orderly way until the last line,
> "Ashes, Ashes (or, A tishoo A tishoo), they all fall down," where
> everyone collapses on the ground. (p. 22[c])

## STAGE OF DEVELOPMENT

We can now view Neumann's second stage of ego development, the magic-phallic, which we consider correlate with EC I, in the context of games of order and disorder. The period begins with the archetypal constellation of what Neumann terms the Separation of the World Parents, and is completed by the first phase of the Hero cycle, the Birth of the Hero. The corresponding levels of ego-consciousness are the polarization of the world into opposites and the first constitution of the independent, anthropomorphic ego. During this period the magic-phallic ego is a fragmentary ego (i.e., intermittent and not yet continuous), its period of constellation depending on the ritual concentration of psychic energy, the latter often occurring in the magic circle of pretense. In the intervals between these episodic structurations the ego returns to the unitary world of *participation mystique* and the primal relationship. Thus the normal state of the ego during EC I is one of fluctuating consciousness, order and disorder. In the newly developed, as yet hardly stabilized bipolar universe, we note again the potential for fluctuation between equilibrium and chaos. A partial list of the opposites discriminated during this period gives us some sense of this fluctuation: ego and not-ego, consciousness and the unconscious (the first reports of dreams); self and world, friendly and unfriendly, good and bad, yes and no; real and pretend, present and past (recall memory appears); and accepting and rejecting, opening and closing.

Erikson's psychosexual modes in EC I, retention and elimination, and the derivative psychosocial modalities, to hold (on) and to let (go), reflect his view of this first confrontation with the opposites. In the nuclear ego crisis of this period, autonomy versus shame and doubt, the fluctuation between constellation and collapse of the emerging ego is again made manifest. We note that this integration is completed when parental persons replace the maternal person as the significant others during this period.

The cognitive world, we discover, is no more stable. Piaget (1962) describes the preconcept, the major cognitive mechanism during this stage of representative intelligence, as follows: "We find one constant characteristic of the 'preconcepts' of this age which seems to be decisive: the child at this stage achieves neither true generality nor true individuality, the notions he uses fluctuating incessantly between the two extremes . . ." (p. 224).

When we transpose this observation to his daughter's developing self-recognition, we are not surprised at Jacqueline's see-saw fluctuation between awareness of self-identity and the lack of self-recognition:

> At [2 years, 11 months, 13 days] J. saw a photograph of herself asleep on my back and leaning against my shoulder (during a mountain walk). She asked anxiously: "*Oh, what's that?* (pointing to herself). *I'm afraid of it.* — But who is it? Can't you see? — *Yes, it's me. Jacqueline's doing this* (imitating the action). *So she's not afraid* (projection on to the photograph)." An hour later she saw the photograph again: "*I'm still a bit afraid.*—But who is it? — *It's me. It's Jacqueline doing this* (imitating)." (p. 224)

In the development of play we again find fluctuation as the norm. The ludic boundaries for EC I are pretend play at 1 to 2 years and imaginative play at 3 to 4 years. As the awareness of make-believe reflects the beginning perception of the symbolic function, the universe is now divided into two spheres, real and pretend. Rosalind Gould (1972) has demonstrated that this new division of the world into the magical and the mundane is a process, not an event. One of the conclusions from her study of the fantasy play of nursery school children is that EC I is a period of "fluctuating certainty," which she defines as "an 'ego-state' that manifests itself in a child's more or less frequent and transient inability to distinguish firmly between a pretend and a real danger" (p. 7). She adds that beyond the age of 4 years the persistence of fluctuating certainty could be viewed as a manifestation of anxiety.

### SANDPLAY TEXT

We can now turn to the worlds made by Bowyer's (1970) five normal subjects aged 2 to 4 years, which she describes as follows (comments in brackets are mine):

They all made worlds so much alike that one had to look for the name on the back of the photograph to identify them [order]. . . . No control was shown by the 2-3-year-olds, i.e., their worlds were chaotic [disorder]. . . . From 3-4 years, however, little islands of coherent detail increased [order]. . . . Children aged 2-3 years did not recognize the edges of the tray as barriers [disorder]. . . . Only a portion of the tray along one horizontal edge—or one edge and a corner . . . had anything placed in it [order and disorder]. (pp. 26-27)

ILLUSTRATIONS

Plates 1 A, B and 2 A, B, C are reproduced from Bowyer (1970). The remainder of the sand worlds illustrating EC I were made by the author's subjects. Note that the ages of some of these children do not fall within the boundary years for this stage (the same is true of some sand world makers in the EC II and MC sections). The discrepancy is minimized not only by the fact that these children are clinical subjects, whom we would expect to exhibit a delay in psychological growth, but by our view of the developmental process as both recapitulative and reconstructive in nature.

*Plates 1 A, B.*  A. World by Jane, age 22 months. Father sits by baby in cot, while mother sweeps the floor. The father, baby, and mother are in relation (order) but have no meaningful connection with the other elements of the tray (disorder). This also applies to the spoon and three vessels. The doll (order) is out of scale and unrelated to the other groupings (disorder). The sand has been acted upon (order) but no pattern is evident, and areas of the tray are left untouched (disorder).

B. Jane's world at age 2 years. Father and mother sit on bench while baby sleeps in the shelter of the tent. This world, made by the same girl two months after the world in Plate 1A, reveals the same general characteristics—coherent combinations of elements which are unrelated to each other, no organization of the whole, and no overall constructive use of sand.

PLATE I A
World of Jane, age 22 months.

PLATE I B
Jane's world at age 2 years.

*Plates 2 A, B, C.* These three sequential trays were made by a
boy 4 years 8 months old.

A. First interview, first world. On the left are a wooden station
with a derailed train, on the right a gun and a cavalryman. The

train and station are in relation (order) but the train is off the track and on its side (disorder). The artillery piece and the mounted military figure are in relation (order) but the horse and rider have fallen (disorder). One can conceive a possible relation between these

PLATE 2A
First world (first interview) of a 4¾-year-old boy.

PLATE 2B
Second world (first interview) of the same boy.

two sets of elements (order) but it is vaguely represented (disorder). There is some attempt at molding the sand into terrain (order) but the results are ill-defined (disorder).

B. First interview, second world. The tray represents a landscape. At the top right, sand has been scooped away to reveal the blue bottom of the tray. There is separation of the earth and the waters (order) but the boundaries are blurred (disorder). The landscape itself (order) is primitively delineated and the form (i.e. whether sea or lake) of the body of water (order) is not clearly represented (disorder).

C. Second interview, only world. A barn, a lawn swing, a fruit and vegetable stand and two houses are grouped appropriately (order) but they are in disarray (disorder). The group of planes at top left and the group of aquanauts around the house at the right (order) are without apparent context (disorder), as is the zoo enclosure at the top right (disorder). There is an impression of a whole (order) but it is poorly integrated (disorder).

PLATE 2C
Third world (next interview) of the same boy.

*Plates 3 A, B.* Two views of a tray made by a 5½-year-old girl in her second visit.

A. There is a mermaid (foreground) and sand scooped away to look like water to the right of center (order) but the mermaid is

PLATE 3A
World of a 5½-year-old girl.

PLATE 3B
Another view of the same world.

partially buried, apparently on land (disorder). There is a division of the earth and waters (order) but the boundaries are unclear (disorder).

B. The tray has been turned so that the water is now in the right foreground and the mermaid to the left. An octopus, which in view A was buried (disorder; Inf II pattern) near the water (order), has been uncovered. The mermaid and octopus are in relation (order).

*Plates 4 A, B.* These two worlds were made during her first visit by a girl 5 years 7 months old.

A. At the top of the picture there is a central group of four horseback riders (order) with one fallen horse and rider (disorder). It is hard to determine whether molding of the sand was to form terrain (order) or was random (disorder).

B. There is a mountain, flatlands, and two bodies of scooped out "water" (order) but these are ill-defined both individually and relationally (disorder). A nearly buried aquanaut (to the left of the closest "pool") is near one of the bodies of water (order) but there is otherwise little context for his presence (disorder). There is a suggestion of overall symmetry and wholeness (order) but it is not a completed integration (disorder).

Finally a description of a sand world not pictured here, which appears to be transitional between EC I and EC II. An 8-year-old girl brought to her interview a bottle containing a grasshopper, which she was planning to "tame" (Mistress of the Beasts). In the dry tray she made a sand world in which a man and a woman (Separation of the World Parents) were moving over the surface of a pond in a canoe (order) while surrounded, above and below the surface of the water/sand by both benign (further order) and threatening (disorder) marine creatures—fish, alligator, turtle, shark, octopus, frog, etc. The man and woman in the canoe on the pond might also be seen as central persons in an EC II configuration. The interview ended with a game of Fish, suggesting progression into Middle Childhood (games with rules).

PLATE 4A
World of a girl 5 years 7 months old (first interview).

PLATE 4B
Another world of the same girl (first interview).

# Early Childhood II (EC II): 3-4 to 6-7 years
## Central-person games
## (Tag)

Neumann's third stage of ego development, the magic-warlike, marks the transition from the matriarchate to the patriarchate. Neumann indicates, however, that development can still be described as a whole because the progression from the matriarchate to the patriarchate applies both to girls and to boys. In the Hero cycle the magic-warlike phase includes the Slaying of the Mother and the Father, which have now become negatively accentuated as the Terrible Mother and the Terrible Father. Neumann (1973) comments as follows:

> This warlike accentuation of the masculine is necessary both phylogenetically and ontogenetically for the liberation of consciousness and the ego from the preponderance of the matriarchate. Only the heroically fighting ego is capable of overcoming the feminine-maternal which, when it impedes the ego and the masculine principle of consciousness in their development toward independence, becomes Terrible Mother, dragon and witch, a source of anxiety. (p. 168)

GAME MODEL

We can now consider the first element in our characterization of the ludic model for EC II, Sutton-Smith's (1972) description of the expressive profile* of the five-year-old, in which we can see the dramatic nature of the central-person imagery of the dragon, witch and monster:

> We may sum up as follows these various approaches to the grammar of the expressive form in dreams, stories, folktales, nursery rhymes and games. In all of these forms as used by children at the

---

*At any level of development the individual's expressive profile is derived from the formal and functional analyses of all the expressive forms (dreams, play, games, drawings, jokes, riddles, etc.) manifest at that particular stage.

age of five, the "flight syndrome" is the key imaginative structure. Furthermore, it is predialectical. It is possible to envisage defeat and failure without adequate counterbalance, although in fully developed folktales there is usually such redress. (p. 532)

Sutton-Smith's second observation suggests that in these same forms we can also observe the transition from the matriarchate to the patriarchate. He continues:

> Judging by the examples in this present study, when the dominance of feminine figures (dreams, stories, folktales) gives way to an equal differentiation of the sexes or predominance of males (play, readers, cartoons), the flight pattern gives way to a fight-flight pattern. To the five-year-old, however, only the active agent (monster or parent figure) and a *submissive* counter agent (child) seem differentiated. Actions involve being attacked, being chased, and escaping; but they do not involve as yet the reciprocals of adequate defense, rescue and capture. (p. 533)

The second element in our characterization of central-person games focuses directly on the transitional nature of this period (Sutton-Smith, 1971c).

> On the basis of an earlier symbolic analysis of children's central-person games . . . these investigators had postulated that these games represent the child's anxieties about exercising independence during the transition from primary to secondary ties. In the course of the game the child can either manifest the endangering independence by running out from a safe base and avoiding a strange person (who is It), or he can retreat to the safety of the home or base. (p. 80)

We can recall from our own playing of tag, Redlight, Mother May I, and King of the Mountain "the variety of ways in which these games configure the relationship between one individual of high power and a number of other individuals of lesser power, thus reflecting the child's own status in relation to adults" (p. 90). Viewed as a progression from games of order and disorder, Sutton-Smith suggests, central-person games reveal "role differentiation to the extent that one or more players have a central role in bringing about the collapse" (p. 22).

STAGE OF DEVELOPMENT

Erikson conceives of this period of development as the play age and defines the nuclear conflict as initiative versus guilt, thus echoing the "warlike accentuation" in the self-assertive, "making" attitude (Erikson, 1963, p. 90). It is also the stage of development when Erikson's basic family (the social reality) becomes internalized as Laing's basic "family" (the psychic reality) (Laing, 1972, pp. 3-19), although it is best known historically as the period of formation of the super-ego, the latter often conceived as monstrously harsh.

In Piaget's accounts of the objective heteronomous morality of EC II, which he contrasts with the subjective autonomous morality of Middle Childhood, we can again discern a central-person pattern. Thus, in explaining the genesis of EC II morality, Piaget (1969) draws on Bovet's concept of "unilateral respect," a sentiment consisting of both affection and fear, which Bovet places at the foundation of the genesis of duty. Piaget writes:

> Affection alone could not suffice to produce obligation, and fear alone provokes only a physical or self-interested submission, but respect involves both affection and fear associated with the position of the inferior in relation to the superior, and therefore suffices to determine the acceptance of orders and consequently the sense of obligation. The sentiment described by Bovet constitutes only one of the two possible forms of respect. We shall call it "unilateral," since it binds an inferior to a superior who is regarded as such, and shall distinguish it from "mutual respect," which is based on reciprocity of esteem. Unilateral respect, if it is indeed the source of the sense of duty, begets in the young child a morality of obedience which is characterized primarily by a *heteronomy* that declines later to make way, at least partially, for the autonomy characteristic of mutual respect. (pp. 123-24)

And, Piaget continues, we find a correspondence in the development of the child's conception of game rules:

> First, in games with rules, children before the age of seven who receive the rules ready-made from their elders (by a mechanism derived from unilateral respect) regard them as "sacred," untouch-

able, and of transcendent origin (parents, the government, God, etc.). Older children, on the contrary, regard rules as the result of agreement among contemporaries, and accept the idea that rules can be changed by means of a democratically arrived at consensus. (p. 127)

Finally, Piaget designates the typical cognitive operation of EC II as semilogic or half logic, which is an operation characterized by its one way direction or lack of reversibility, as demonstrated in the child's ability to understand the relationship many-to-one, and lack of ability to construct a valid classification system based on the relationships of one-to-many. It is only at the completion of EC II that the child will be able to unite two classes, e.g. fathers united with mothers to constitute parents.

The ludic markers for this stage are fantasy play at 3 to 4 years and social play with peer playmates at about 6 to 7 years. One play phenomenon worthy of special note is the imaginary character (the beginning of fictional narrative) and the imaginary companion which, in one form or another, become central figures in the child's life, often undergoing a variety of progressive transformations (Piaget, 1962, pp. 129-31; Ames and Learned, 1946; Thompson and Johnson, 1973).

### SANDPLAY TEXT

We can now project our explanatory ludic pattern into a series of sand worlds.

### ILLUSTRATIONS

Plates 5 A, B, C are reproduced from Bowyer (1970). The rest of the trays used to illustrate EC II were made by the author's subjects.

*Plates 5 A, B, C.* A. World of a 4-year-old boy, showing the zoo and station near his home, a policeman in control, and many dishes for food. According to Bowyer it is typical of the age group in its inclusion of undifferentiated traffic signs and a policeman (superego?). Both the policeman assemblage and the penned animal reveal the EC II central-person configuration, as well as certain characteristics of EC I (order and disorder).

B. In this world of another 4-year-old boy, the policeman has been replaced by cowboys in control and the alligator by many

PLATE 5A
World of a 4-year-old boy.

PLATE 5B
World of a 4-year-old boy.

closely penned cattle. The aeroplane, Bowyer notes, was a recurring object (a masculine symbol?) in this boy's worlds.

C. In a quite different way, this world made by a 7-year-old boy also manifests the central-person patterning. At different times this

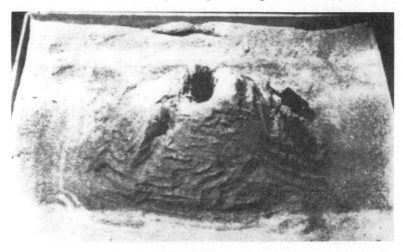

PLATE 5C
World of a 7-year-old boy.

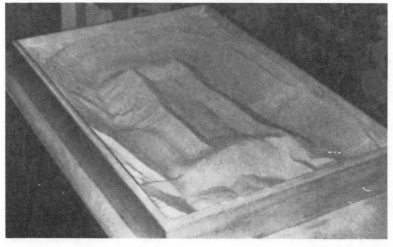

PLATE 5D
World of a 5½-year-old boy (first interview).

configuration was explained to Bowyer as a hole being made in the courtyard to search for coal, Mount Everest, and a volcano.

*Plate 5 D.* This sand world was made by a 5½-year-old boy during his first interview. Its ordered simplicity in the absence of evident disorder suggests that it may be transitional from EC I to EC II. The central rectangular structure is carefully contoured as is the oval surround, while its indeterminate nature invites speculation—a mesa, an altar, a temple, etc. These images suggest the abode of a central person.

*Plates 6 A, B.* Two views of the same world made by a 5½-year-old girl during her first interview.

A. In the first view the central person is not visible but is implied in the empty corner of a quaternity of figures surrounding a pool. Occupying the other three corners are two mermaids, a standing Indian, and two Indians in a canoe. In the narrative accompanying her tray the girl said that there was "a diver at the bottom of the pool."

B. In the second view the "diver at the bottom of the pool" has been uncovered (by the therapist). In this burying there may be the recapitulation of an Inf II theme at the EC II level.

*Plates 7 A, B.* These are two views of the same sand world made by a boy 6 years 4 months old, during his first interview.

A. The haloed face of a chthonic monster is emerging from the center of the sandtray.

B. Its graphic quality suggests the depiction of a nocturnal dream monster, ogre, or dragon.

*Plates 8 A, B, C.* An overall view and details of the first tray made by a girl 7 years 10 months old.

A. Our attention is immediately drawn to the windowless block-house with its reinforced roof.

B. Removal of the roof discloses the central figure of a monstrous, pent pachyderm.

C. With the roof of the barn removed we can see a circle of young animals with the more benign figure of a baby giraffe as the central animal.

PLATE 6A
World of a 5½-year-old girl (first interview).

PLATE 6B
Another view of the same world.

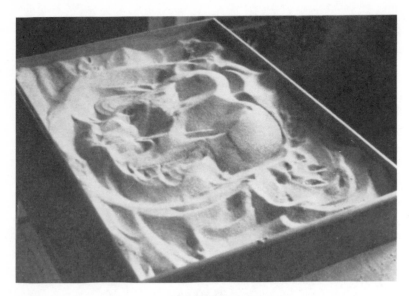

PLATE 7A
World of a boy 6 years 4 months old.

PLATE 7B
Another view of the same world showing the "face."

PLATE 8A
World of a girl 7 years 10 months old.

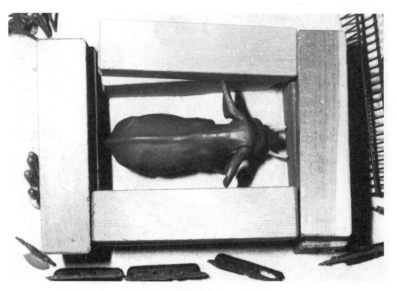

PLATE 8B
Detail of same world. The blockhouse with its roof removed.

PLATE 8C
Detail of the barn with its roof removed.

PLATE 8D
Another world of the same girl.

*Plate 8 D.* The same girl made this more abstract rendering of the EC II pattern, a central vessel surrounded by spherical satellites.

*Plates 9 A, B.* These are views of the first sand world made by a boy 11 years 8 months old.

A. In this view it is apparent that the primary direction of a massive attack by cavalry, infantry, animals, and machines is toward the central house, although there are scattered instances of centrifugal movement (a lion, lower left, and an alligator, top right).

B. Removal of the roof of the house reveals the lone central person, a pirate, toward whom the weapons are directed.

*Plate 9 C.* The first world of a boy one month before his 12th birthday. The heroic central figure stands on an island, which itself has been placed in the center of the tray.

PLATE 9A
First world of a boy 11 years 8 months old.

PLATE 9B
Detail of the same world with the roof of the house removed.

PLATE 9C
First world of a boy almost 12.

# Middle Childhood (MC): 6–7 to 11–12 years
## Games of peer sexual differentiation
## (Jacks, Marbles)

Two studies of sex differences in the symbolic play of children in MC provide a natural transition to games of peer sexual differentiation, our ludic explanatory model for this period. The first of these is Erikson's classic paper *Sex Differences in the Play Configurations of Preadolescents* (1951), which directs our attention to the sex differences in MC as manifested in the symbolic play of 11-, 12- and 13-year-old girls and boys. Erikson reported differences in both the form and the content of the dramatic play of his subjects.

> It will be seen that girls, on the whole, tend to build quiet scenes of everyday life, preferably within a home or in a school. The most frequent "exciting scene" built by girls is a quiet family constellation, in a house without walls, with the older girl playing the piano. Disturbances, in the girls' scenes, are primarily caused by animals, usually cute puppies, or by mischievous children—always boys. More serious accidents occur too, but there are no murders and there is little gun play. The boys have the upper hand in street and outdoor scenes, and especially in scenes with wild animals, Indians, or automobile accidents; they prefer toys which move or represent motion. Peaceful scenes are predominantly traffic scenes under the guiding supervision of the policeman. In fact, the policeman is the "person" most often used by the boys, while the older girl is the one preferred by girls. (p. 671)

> The most significant sex differences in the use of the play space, then, add up to the following picture: in the boys, the outstanding variables are height and downfall, and motion and its channelization and arrest (policeman); in girls, static interiors, which are open, simply enclosed, or blocked and intruded upon. (p. 688)

The second paper is a recent study intended to repeat and extend Erikson's findings. Cramer and Hogan (1975) replicated Erikson's results in 22 girls and 25 boys with an average age of 11 years 5 months, the range being 9 years 8 months to 12 years 10 months.

They also discovered sex differences in the play of the younger children in their study, 22 girls and 23 boys, the average age being 5 years 6 months, with a range of 3 years 7 months to 6 years 3 months. "There were clear differences in the initial selection of play materials, boys choosing blocks, vehicles, and male uniformed dolls, while girls chose furniture, domestic animals, family dolls, and female uniformed dolls" (p. 151).

### GAME MODEL

The games reflecting these differences have been described in research directed toward sexual categorization in game preferences as determined both by play scales and play participation. Sutton-Smith and Savasta (Schwartzman, 1978) have reviewed a number of these studies covering the age period of 5 to 12 years and have summarized these investigations as follows:

> For males games may be an exercise in power tactics but . . . for females they generally are not. . . . The games preferred by boys show a greater emphasis on bodily strength and bodily contact, the use of larger spaces, for success achieved through active interference in the other play activities, for well-defined outcomes in which winners and losers are clearly labelled, for games permitting individual initiative, for a continuous flow of activity, for motor activity involving the whole body, for players acting simultaneously or in concert. Any type of sport could be taken to exemplify these dimensions. Girls for their part show a greater interest in games where turns are taken in ordered sequence, where there is choral activity, song and rhyme, verbalism, where rhythm is involved, where the stages in play are multiple but well defined, where competition is indirect, where there is a multiplicity of rules dictating every move, where only parts of the body are involved and where there is much solitary practice, where there is competition between individuals rather than groups. The games of hopscotch, jump rope and jackstones are good examples. (p. 112)

We can expand our list of paradigmatic games for MC by presenting part of the game preference scales developed by Rosenberg and Sutton-Smith (1964, p. 260).

| *Masculinity* | *Femininity* |
|---|---|
| bandits | dolls |
| soldiers | dressing up |
| cowboys | houses |
| cops and robbers | store |
| cars | school |
| marbles | actors |
| bows and arrows | actresses |
| . . . | . . . |
| shooting | hopscotch |
| fish | jump rope |
| hunt | jacks |
| make radio | sewing |
| model aeroplane | cooking |

## STAGE OF DEVELOPMENT

We have been denied Neumann's completed view of this stage of ego development, the solar-warlike, as the following passage by his editor (Neumann, 1973) explains: "The author did not live to complete the present work. It ends in the middle of the section concerning the relation between the Self, the father archetype and the super-ego and it does not reach the stage of development at which the girl child requires separate treatment" (pp. 202-03). We do know, however, that Neumann designated the solar-warlike stage as the period when the emerging hero-ego identifies itself with the father archetype. He also indicated that it was at this point that the sexes begin to diverge in their development and that a girl begins to differ from a boy in her psychology.

Turning briefly to Piaget (1962), we are not surprised to find that, as a reflection of his interest in the educational process, he emphasizes the features shared in common by all children in this period. He notes the correspondence in MC between the reversibility of the cognitive operations and the mutuality of the social co-operations characteristic of this stage, the latter established in part by adapted speech. In his theory of ludic development, Piaget (1962) defines games with rules as typical of MC: "Unlike symbols, rules necessarily imply social or inter-individual relationships. . . . Rules are a regulation imposed by the group, and their violation carries a sanction" (pp. 112-13).

The ludic boundaries, then, for MC are social play with peer playmates at 6 to 7 years and team play with teammates at about 11 to 12 years. We are in the familiar arena of the school or neighborhood playground which most of us can recall, with jump rope here, aggies and steelies there, and the inevitable skirmishes in between.

SANDPLAY TEXT

We will now examine a series of worlds made by the author's subjects, in which female and male trays are in marked contrast. (The worlds illustrated are representative of the MC sample, which constituted my largest data base.) It is worth noting that although Bowyer makes no mention of sex differences in the world constructions made by the normal 7- through 11-year-olds in her study, we will see that her descriptions of these worlds reveal close sexual similarities both in content and configuration with the worlds that follow.

These MC worlds, in addition to differences between them attributable to sexual identity, are characterized by a greater overall integration compared to those that illustrated the earlier stages of childhood development.

ILLUSTRATIONS

*Plates 10 A, B.* A comparison between (A) the tray of a girl 7 years 10 months old and (B) the tray of an 8-year-old boy.

A. The girl's world depicts an Edenic setting, albeit with two threatening reptiles (alligator and snake, right foreground), in which two hula maidens (center picture) dance to ukulele music.

B. In striking contrast, the boy nearly the same age has constructed a battle scene between two opposing armies, with dead and wounded figures in evidence.

*Plates 11 A, B.* The next pair of trays were made by (A) a girl 9 years 7 months old and (B) a 9-year-old boy.

A. The girl has constructed a peaceful farm scene, with separate groups of animal families (e.g. pigs, cattle, ducks) under the

PLATE 10A
World of a girl 7 years 10 months old.

PLATE 10B
World of an 8-year-old boy.

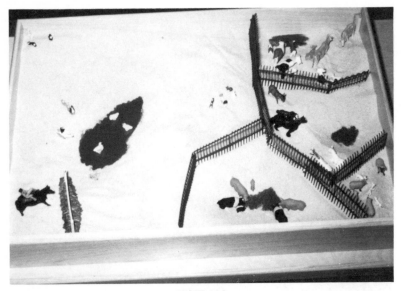

PLATE IIA
World of a girl 9 years 7 months old.

PLATE IIB
World of a 9-year-old boy.

watchful eye of their farmer (mounted, bottom left corner).

B.  In sharp contrast, her male peer has depicted a surging forest battle marked by several instances of hand-to-hand combat.

Bowyer notes that from 7 to 8 years onward, and in adulthood, there are individual differences, some subjects at each age making peaceful farm scenes rather than warlike ones. She also observed that from 5 to 10 years fencing increased, often used without gates at the younger stages; for normal subjects ten years seemed to be a peak period for fencing.

*Plates 12 A, B.* The first of these worlds (A) was made by a 9¾-year-old girl while the second (B) was constructed by a boy exactly one year younger.

A.  The girl's tray depicts a peaceful Indian village, with domestic activities near the teepee, a pow-wow near the totem pole, and nearby braves (bottom left in canoe and top right with bow) fishing and hunting.

PLATE 12A
World of a 9¾-year-old girl.

B. Her male counterpart has illustrated the start of a classic American battle between the cowboys (foreground) and the Indians.

Bowyer observed that from 7+ the Indian and Cowboy theme appears, and so do opposing armies spatially arranged; there is increasingly clear differentiation of the different forces.

*Plates 13 A, B.* These seascapes are by (A) a 9¾-year-old girl and (B) a boy 10 years 5 months old.

A. The girl has depicted Ondine's realm, with two mermaids in close interaction (top right), a third mermaid playing in the sand (mid left side), and all three surrounded by their watery minions.

B. The boy has constructed a naval battle which is being waged in the air with airplanes, on the sea by ships, and under the water by frogmen (center foreground and upper right) and a submarine.

PLATE 12B
World of an 8¾-year-old boy.

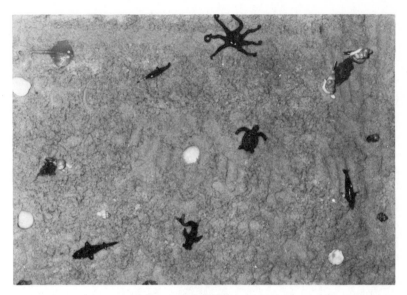

PLATE I3A
Seascape of a 9¾-year-old girl.

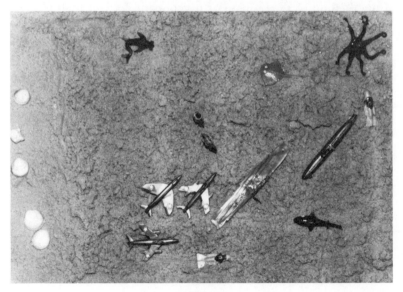

PLATE I3B
Seascape of a boy 10 years 5 months old.

# Conclusions

In the preceding pages we have proposed a method for the epigenetic analysis of sandplay constructions, and illustrated its paradigmatic application to four stages of development in the first twelve years of life. The limitations in this presentation, of course, are almost too numerous to specify: the number of subjects is small, and "clinical" trays have been used to suggest normative patterns; other deficits are the absence of material illustrating the stages of development in adolescence and adulthood, and the lack of data demonstrating the hierarchical recapitulation, reconstruction, and integration at all stages. The method will also gain in validity when correlations have been established between its analyses of play configurations and the results of analyses of other expressive behaviors (dreams, drawings, etc.) along the lines of the expressive profile. One immediate necessity is the further extension of the method to the domain of psychopathology at each level of development.

We have presented the method, however, in spite of these limitations, in the hope that it will be of sufficient interest and potential usefulness for the limitations themselves to become occasions for subsequent studies. The methodological gap in respect to the analysis of sandplay configurations is obvious, and innovation, we suggest, is the necessary continuing response. If, as has been theorized, play is a major growth center of the psyche, second perhaps only to dreams in this respect, then the general significance of our work is firmly established.

# Developmental Stages
# in Children's Sand Worlds

KATHERINE BRADWAY

In viewing children's sand worlds I have found it helpful to relate them to the stages of ego development propounded by Erich Neumann (1973) as five stages and by Dora Kalff (1971) as three stages. Neumann distinguishes the first stage as the "phallic-chthonian" stage whose vegetative and animal form is passive. "It has not yet freed itself from the dominance of the matriarchal power of nature and the unconscious" (p. 139). Neumann speaks of the next two stages as the "magic-phallic" and the "magic-warlike," which are differentiated from the first stage by the activity of the ego. He continues:

> It is the magic-warlike ego that first overcomes its dependence on the matriarchate, so much so that it effects the transition to the patriarchate with which the ensuing "solar ego" is correlated. In the solar-warlike phase, the ego identifies itself with the father archetype. It is followed by the solar-rational stage of the adult patriarchal ego, whose independence culminates in relative freedom of the will. . . . (p. 139)

Kalff's experience coincided with Neumann's theory and led her to propose three stages of ego development: animal-vegetative, fighting, and adaptation to the collective (p. 24).

In studying the sandplay productions of children 6, 9, and 12 years old, I have found Kalff's three successive stages represented in initial sand worlds of children at each of these age levels.

PLATE I
First world of a 6-year-old boy: the animal-vegetative stage.

Plate 1, the first sand world of a 6-year-old boy, is an example of the animal-vegetative stage made up exclusively of animals and plant life. All of the animals used by this youngster are prehistoric. Children use prehistoric animals more frequently than do adults, and their use seems to be more consistent with the chthonic character of this stage than does the use of domesticated animals. The dark area right of center is a "water hole" made by scraping the sand away from the dark blue floor of the tray. Many children provide sources of water, and also food, for the animals they place in the sandtray. I perceive this as an experience of giving to one's self, which is a step toward actively obtaining self-nourishment and thus a step toward a higher level of ego autonomy. The addition of trees and plants to sand worlds may appear at any age level. The inclusion of plant life seems to be related to an inner sense of potential for psychological growth, in contrast to the starkness of sand worlds that connote feelings of lifelessness.

There is a large mound just left of the center of this boy's scene with four smaller less visible mounds in other parts of the tray. His

PLATE 2
First world of a 9-year-old boy: the fighting stage.

identifying these mounds as volcanoes, even forming craters in the center of each one, suggests pent-up feelings. As these feelings emerge they can propel the youngster from the passive matriarchate recognized by Neumann into the active fighting stage at the beginning of the patriarchal sequence of stages. As might be anticipated then, the next two worlds of this boy were dominated by fighting. The first of these was a war between soldiers of two countries. The second involved a king protected by many guards, suggesting the emergence of the archetypal masculine (just as for a girl the use of a queen may coincide with the emergence of the archetypal feminine). This boy seems well into the transition to the patriarchate discussed by Neumann.

A 9-year-old boy's first world (Plate 2) skips the animal-vegetative stage and illustrates the fighting stage of ego development. His next two worlds were also depictions of fighting; the first of them personalized the battle between him and me. Children at this stage often engage the therapist as an adversary in the drama depicted, or demand their adversive involvement through testing limits by,

PLATE 3
First world of a 12-year-old girl:
the stage of adaptation to the collective.

for example, "letting" sand go over the sides of the tray onto the floor. A later development may consist of a joint creation initiated by the child. The negative and positive approaches of the child toward the therapist usually alternate with some regularity as the child develops.

The third fighting scene of this boy consisted of a "war over a baby," which may have symbolized conflict over, or ambivalence regarding, a new development in himself. The inclusion of a well in this latter scene suggested the obtaining of nourishment or energy from below the earth—from the unconscious—to aid in the resolution of the conflict. Fences introduced in his two following worlds would seem to reflect the recognition of the need for restrictions or controls associated with further ego development, possibly related to his "shooting" of the therapist in the second session and the new development announced by the appearance of the baby in the third session.

The first world of a 12-year-old girl (Plate 3) skips the animal-vegetative and fighting stages and seems to be representative of

Kalff's third stage, adaptation to the collective. I have found that children's use of fences coincides with their emerging ability to "confront and be confronted by the outer forces of culture," as Kalff describes this stage. Other indications of this stage appear to be depictions of school; contests such as sporting events; interactions—especially conflictual—with authority figures (parents, teachers, police); contrasts between good and bad. The period of transition, which may last for several weeks or months, is often marked by the alternation between scenes of fighting and scenes of animals enclosed in fences. Frequently, in viewing a sequence of a child's worlds, one can accurately predict when a scene with enclosed animals will occur by the appearance in the preceding session of marked aggression.

Sources of energy often appear during the period of transition. It is as if the ego needs an additional supply of energy in order to cope with the struggle between inner and outer forces. Another object used during this period, although not solely in this period, is the bridge, which indicates an attempt to make connections between opposing parts of one's self; the good and the bad, the passive and the aggressive, the grown-up self and the baby self, the compliant and the rebellious, the masculine and the feminine. The recognition of and tolerance for opposites, followed by a resolution, is accompanied by a transformation in the psyche, and the bridge seems to denote the potential for making a connection and for eventual integration between opposing parts of one's self. The parts may or may not be decisively delineated. Sometimes the bridge is set into the tray without its being clear how it serves to "connect." But its symbolic value as a connector is still valid.

Returning to the 12-year-old girl whose first world is presented in Plate 3, we can see some characteristics of this transition to the stage of adaptation to the collective. In her initial world the fences are placed around farmyard animals. This is not a scene restricting potentially violent aggression, as fences around tigers and lions would be, but it is indicative of the child's experiencing the need for restrictions in connection with her instincts. One of the farmgirls with the animals is feeding them by scattering grain. The nourishing of animals as a symbolic giving to one's self, and hence a step toward ego independence, was suggested in connection with the 6-year-old boy's first world. The greater activity of scattering grain as compared with providing water holes may be viewed as related to the higher level of development of the 12-year-old. A second possibility not previously mentioned is the possible link between the feeding of animals and nurturing as a feminine value.

A second girl in the fenced area of the scene is milking a cow. This is a more direct depiction of obtaining self-nourishment, since it does not require identifying an animal as part of one's self; the 12-year-old merely needs to identify with a girl figure like herself. There is an additional point to be made: the negative aspects of instincts, implied in the need to restrict them, are balanced by the positive aspects, implied in their furnishing nourishment. And so, the full circle: one nourishes one's instinctual side; one obtains nourishment from one's instinctual side.

Nourishment or energy from a deeper level, from under the earth, from the unconscious, is depicted by the well in the lower right corner. A male figure near the well is carrying buckets balanced on a pole across his shoulders, apparently on his way to get some water, one more depiction of actively obtaining nourishment.

On the left side of the scene are representations of masculine and feminine. At the top a man and woman are standing by a house which has a car on the road in front of it. The house, a feminine symbol, is separated from the car, a masculine symbol, by pebbles marking the roadway. Lower on the left side a man on a horse is approaching a bridge. The car and horse are inanimate and animate forms respectively of transportation energy, a more dynamic level of energy than is nourishment. The bridge, as suggested earlier, indicates an attempt to make connections between parts of one's self. The identity of the presently opposing parts that might eventually be connected is not clear here, but the several representations and symbols of masculinity and femininity, as well as the contrast between nourishment and locomotion, provide clues.

PLATE 4
The girl's final world: further development of the same stage.

The 12-year-old's next two worlds both showed a diving girl going into water, an activity providing a more direct access to the unconscious than obtaining water from a well; and both scenes showed gasoline stations, which represent a supplier of energy for locomotion. Her fourth and final world (Plate 4) shows further development of adaptation to the collective. Two sections are devoted to sporting contests: "Olympic gymnastics" as she called them, and six racing bicyclists. A third section consists of a schoolroom in which four children are seated at their desks and one is interacting directly with the teacher and the principal. In a fourth section of this scene is the diving girl. In retrospect I might interpret this third appearance of the diving girl as a readiness for this 12-year-old to continue into more extensive psychotherapy, but circumstances did not lead to further sessions with her.

Although there is a relation between chronological age and appearance of successive stages, as suggested by the foregoing discussion, the relationship is of course not a perfect one. Nor is the progression from one stage to the next a rigidly fixed sequence. The examples and discussion are not meant to suggest an invariable course of development, but rather to aid in identifying the stages of ego development proposed by Neumann and Kalff and to illustrate their use in understanding sandplay productions. This kind of understanding is not necessarily communicated to the child in words. In fact, I avoid making interpretations to the child during the ongoing process of sandplay in favor of spontaneous nonverbal communication. I think an appreciation of what the sand worlds are depicting and an empathy for the struggles and the achievements which the child encounters are conducive to providing the *temenos* (Kalff's "free and sheltered space") within which development will occur. A joint viewing with the child of projected slides of his or her sand world series provides the opportunity to exchange observations of what has happened and at that time cognition can beneficially join feeling experience.

# The Use of Sandplay
# with Men

KAREN A. SIGNELL

The purpose of this paper is to discuss and illustrate the use of sandplay with adult male patients. Since I am writing from the vantage point of a woman, I have supplemented my experience with ideas from male colleagues. (For instance, my analytic colleagues John Beebe and Neil Russack urged that I give "equal time" to the father complex, which is generally neglected in Jungian literature in favor of the mother complex, and this I have tried to do.)

The first part of this paper describes issues in introducing sandplay to men. The next part is devoted to two cases with prominent father complexes. The third deals with mistakes that can arise in using the sandtray in therapy, and instances where its use may even be inadvisable.

## Introducing the Sandtray

It is my impression that sandplay is under-utilized with men patients and I have wondered why. I think one reason is that men in our culture have reservations about "play" or "performance," and hence might hesitate to use the sandtray. I have noticed that female

Jungian analysts utilize sandplay in their practice more than male analysts do, and this imbalance suggests that there may actually be more use of sandplay with women patients as well. When Clare Thompson (Note 8) made a survey of the literature on sandplay she found that the ratio of women authors to men was 3 to 1.

Imaginative play is largely denied men in our achievement-oriented culture. Play itself and non-professional art—art merely "for fun," private, pleasurable and self-expressive—such activities belong to the "women's sphere." For that reason I think sandplay can be important for some men—a rare opportunity for loosening up and experiencing the free flow of feelings, imagination, and life force that comes with the interplay of conscious and unconscious.

An analyst might want to consider, then, how sandplay could be made equally accessible to men. To make it socially acceptable, I sometimes tell patients how Jung discovered the usefulness of sandplay for himself. It was during his depression, after separating from Freud, that he found himself playing with objects on the shores of the lake, as he had in boyhood. He discovered that it was profoundly useful to him in giving form to his inner experience and working through his depression. For the patient, Jung's experience offers a dignified model and conveys the potential usefulness of sandplay.

On the other hand it is important for the patient to acknowledge his initial doubts and skepticism about the medium. Sometimes I recount my own initial reaction: "When my analyst first introduced me to the sandtray, I thought 'Bah-humbug!' But if she had moved one of the objects in the sandtray I'd just done, I'd have shot her!"

What I consider most important is that the patient rely on his sense of inner readiness to encounter the unconscious. Using the sandtray is a subtle process, and one needs to place faith in one's own experience of its value. In my analytic practice with men and women I have found that about half of my patients never use the sandtray; others do a sandtray once every year or two; and some use it a few times a year or more. My adult patients, then, call upon this resource on fairly rare occasions, to get a bearing on their inner state of affairs.

. The patient's attitude in approaching sandplay is crucial. I think it requires a seriousness of purpose, a sense of play, and waiting for the right time. Sometime early in therapy I mention the sandtray (easily visible across the room) then wait for the patient's inner prompting; or I invite someone to use it when the time seems ripe.

It is not enough to do a sandtray because one is "willing to try it." This suggests too light an approach, from a puer position (pleasing the mother) or positive transference position (pleasing the therapist). It takes more commitment than that. I think of how the Celtic hero Culhwch (Layard, 1975) could not begin his quest until he had enlisted the aid of Eiddoel (his detached, intellectual side) who was imprisoned on his lofty crag in self-imposed exile from life. So, too, a person's ego alliance must be won so that he can put the ego's strength and persistence behind this kind of movement in his psyche. Consequently I convey to the patient my deep respect for the subtle process of active imagination—the activity in which ego, unconscious and self meet—and for the great effort it takes to allow the process to happen freely. Again people often need and deserve explanations, so sometimes I explain the sandplay process as "a three-dimensional picture of one's psyche at this time," "working through inner material," or "similar to a waking dream, letting conscious and unconscious interact."

I often find it necessary to talk with patients (especially men who have been denied opportunities to play or to acknowledge their unconscious) about the "spirit of play," the creative spirit, and the gifts that come when we allow an atmosphere for the unconscious to come forth (Aite, 1978).* To encourage this spirit, the sandtray is on the floor, so that a person kneels or sits on a mat in a relaxed fashion, similar to the way we played as children.

Since many patients have experienced an intrusive or judgmental parent, they need to be left alone during the sandplay process. (This is especially true for men who have a strong need for separateness.) The patient and his psyche need to be allowed center

---

*See also Louis H. Stewart, "Play and Sandplay," this volume p. 21.

stage, with the analyst in the wings. I sit a few feet to a patient's side and a little behind, where he can hardly see me out of the corner of his eye and yet can sense my presence nearby. However, I feel deeply *with* the person throughout the sandplay process as a "container" (providing a safe therapeutic context). After my brief direction, "Let your hands just move the sand, if you want, and put any objects in it that you feel drawn toward," I sit back in silence, except for briefly acknowledging any comment that might be made. After the patient is finished I move up a little to talk, as he shares it with me, but still remain at some distance because this is *his* territory.

In my view, the sandplay process is largely a product of the unconscious, with the conscious ego lightly guiding and helping it take form. Some integration between ego and unconscious takes place, subtly and nonverbally, during the sandplay process itself. Afterward, the observing ego, as a more separate and detached entity, relates to the completed sand world in a more direct, conceptual, or verbal way. When working with a patient, therefore, I do not think it is necessary to do a great deal of interpretation or to seek intellectual understanding of what happened. For the most part the sandplay experience stands on its own. On the other hand, it is often useful to interpret and understand it to some degree. Usually the patient and I do some amplification, as in dreamwork, staying in the twilight world between conscious and unconscious, and trusting the intuitions and insights that come to consciousness from "walking around" the material. Beaming too bright a light of consciousness on the sand world can impede the flow of spontaneity for future sandplay, and it is by remaining quietly receptive that we can hear and see what the unconscious has to convey to us.

However, so that the experience does not slip back into the unconscious, with the patient's permission I take Polaroid pictures after the session, and give one to him the next time we meet. This allows chance for further thoughts to emerge and sometimes sandplay themes naturally weave into dream material, or what is currently happening in a patient's life.

PLATE I
Sandtray objects.

## SANDPLAY OBJECTS

Therapists unfamiliar with working with men in sandplay therapy may be interested in knowing what sandplay objects men feel drawn toward. In surveying men's sand worlds I have found certain *general categories* important: (1) *Nature objects* (such as moss for shrubs, thorns for thickets) to show men's almost forgotten relationship to the vegetative Earth Mother, that is, the growth and replenishment that comes with quiet waiting, not volition and movement. (2) *Found objects* from the ground or beach (such as weather-beaten clothes pins, old pieces of iron). Men like to construct their own sandtray objects—bridges and so forth. (3) *Ethnic artifacts* (such as ancient clay gods and goddesses, Native American totems, mythic Asian figures) as alternatives to objects already designated in our culture to signify certain archetypes. These permit the patient's unconscious, rather than his intellect, to choose, and offer a way to express the strangeness or distant quality of an archetype. (4) *Jungle animals* (especially monkeys, big predators) to express relationship to instincts and aggression.

Certain *specific objects* from my collection (Plate 1) are important and frequently used in men's sand worlds: (1) *Young Krishna* offering the sphere. This is a hopeful sign in a person's sandplay—the Divine Child and his promise. It means to me that a patient is deeply committed to the analytic process and the self. (2) *Scallop shells.* These express a relationship to the positive feminine, specifically the open, containing element. (3) *The Golden Throne.* This figure is important in men's sand worlds in showing their *position* in relationship to the Father archetype, the outer world and authority. Important in men's psychology are (a) their position in relation to their father and siblings; (b) their position among men or in society (a proper relationship to being ruled or ruling, and submitting to the old order or establishing a new one); and (c) the position of divine sonship or kingship (a relation to higher values, to the meaning and mystery of life). (4) *The blue sphere.* This is often used to represent the "treasure" beyond material things. In a man's sandplay it occurs in a masculine context in relation to the sky, so I do not think it represents his anima or feminine side, but rather his masculine spirit.

I would also recommend therapists working with men to include the following objects in their sandplay collection: figures of old men, a bird in flight, snakes, a sun and moon, a feather, an egg, a beast of burden (camel, donkey, or horse with a pack), and a silver or white female (anima) figure.

# Therapeutic Purpose of Sandplay for Patient and Therapist

In this and the following section I will describe and illustrate the therapeutic benefit of sandplay for men (although much of what I have to say holds true for women, too). The main value of sandplay for the patient is that it is a way to give form to his unconscious. Through sandplay he can *see* something happening in his inner life and be aware in a concrete way of the reality of the psyche. It is a surprise to him to look at his completed world and see how autonomously and creatively his unconscious has functioned.

For the man who is cut off from his unconscious (e.g. who has no dreams) sandplay can make available to him unconscious images and affects. Or there are men who have dreams and dutifully type them up but despite their best intentions somehow maintain the *status quo,* resisting new ideas that might spring from the unconscious or selectively interpreting dreams to fit their preconceptions. For these men, whose dreams remain under tight ego dominance keeping the transcendent function* at bay, sandplay offers an alternative. They cannot prepare it beforehand, nor provide a product, as in painting. There are no norms for "good" sand worlds. Sandplay is an active experience of the unconscious, relatively free of ego dominance.

A patient in therapy is in the position of reporting past experiences—his dreams or life events, so therapy consists largely of the verbal, what can be put into words. By its very nature it largely confines a man to being passive, observational, intellectual, and distant from his material. One refreshing exception in therapy is direct interaction with the therapist—real life encounters, transference relations, and subtle nonverbal communication between patient and therapist. Sandplay offers another exception. It allows the patient to interact directly, nonverbally, with his inner world in the presence of another person. He can share an emotional experience vivid in images. Moreover, it is an experience that is confirmed by another person, and therefore hard to discount or let slip back into the unconscious.

---

*The transcendent function can be described as a spontaneous transformation of energy arising from the resolution of the tension between opposite forces. It represents an inner process of having integrated conscious and unconscious contents of the psyche. It results in new energy, new perspective, new possibilities.

For the therapist, sandplay helps in various ways. Of course certain sand worlds, like "big dreams," stand out in a man's analysis. Perhaps he is in the midst of a complex, and in the sand world it can be seen in full and vivid detail, given outer expression by his own specific array of personal images and affect. Thereafter both patient and therapist have a common way to refer to the complex and the specific forms it takes—for instance, "the woman with the blue-tangled hair," or "the iron pot," instead of more general (and possibly inaccurate) designations such as "the mother complex."

There are three main ways in which I find sandplay helpful in understanding a patient:

*(1) Prognostic sandtrays.* Sometimes, as with dreams, a man's sand worlds are prospective—showing the path that lies ahead. Paths are prominent in men's sand worlds, as in their dreams and in the myths of male heroes. The reason is that to become a man, a male has to acquire the identity of the "other." He needs to be different. Psychologically, he must leave his mother, strike out on his own, and do something different to prove himself.

Sometimes a man is aware that a particular sand world is a journey across land, water, or desert; it may incorporate traveling by boat, walking, and so on. Sometimes, however, he has no conscious idea of the journey content of his sand world, and then it helps for the therapist to know how to recognize it. The journey world occurs early, among a man's first sand worlds. It looks different from the more typical adult sand world organized into clusters of objects or dynamic opposites, or at least around a focal point. Instead, its objects are apparently scattered at random all over the sandtray. A distinctive feature often present is a curving line meandering through the sandtray, going near objects. I understand this as letting go sufficiently of the ego's straightline thinking to follow the circuitous route of the unconscious. Both modes interact back and forth to make a snake-like movement (see Figure 1) that sometimes roughly forms a large circle.

I think there is intrinsic value in a man's getting in touch with his inner plan (and knowing at least that there *is* one), even though the

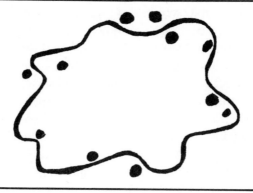

FIGURE I

specific meaning may remain obscure to him and the therapist until it unfolds in the course of time.

*(2) Developmental Stages.* Sandplay provides an opportunity for a man to work through a normal developmental conflict, or to consolidate a gain by registering it in the sandtray. I find these visible nodal points useful in understanding where a patient is psychologically.*

*(3) Working through Conflicts.* Sandplay offers an active arena where a man can struggle with conflicts of opposites, that is "do something," sometimes bringing about a resolution. This use resembles Freudian play therapy, but without the necessity of interpretation or emphasis on abreaction alone. Men patients are often facing choices, partly because of the choices open to them, and partly because of the importance of the Father archetype in their lives, with its connotations of decision and authority. There are times when a man is torn between opposites, must make a decision to do this or that, and he plays out the drama in the sandtray

---

*As I demonstrate in "The Sandplay Process in One Man's Development," this volume p. 157, a series of sand worlds is usually necessary to see where a man is moving in his development.

by allowing the unconscious to move figures to new positions. The result is a moving picture, rather than a static one.

On occasion, when a man is stymied in an analytic hour, I may suggest sandplay, and trust that the interplay of the conscious and unconscious can bring out fresh juxtapositions and the possibility of change. I recall when a patient was obsessed with suicidal thoughts and nothing seemed to help. As an analyst, I was afraid to "let the unconscious loose" at this juncture, but despite our fear we both decided to risk it. The patient found himself acting out a drama in the sandtray. After an initial regressive profane image, a human figure emerged in the sandtray and went to the middle of the Golden Gate Bridge. The figure could not bring himself to jump, nor could he get to the land on the other side. Finally, after a long, intense struggle, a resolution occurred (the figure took the courage to swim across the channel); after that the patient's suicidal thoughts subsided. I think it was important to him that he could go through such overwhelming feelings, the initial disintegration, conflict, and resolution, with another human being participating and sharing with him, so that he might find strength by going to the bottom of his anger and helplessness.

The two cases to be presented next also reflect major points of choice in men's lives, and illustrate "working through" in sandplay.

## Case Study: Sam

The first case illustrates how a man can work through aspects of the father complex in sandplay. The patient, whom I will call Sam, had a father who was a "tyrant at home, and timid at work." One of Sam's main problems was being too aggressive. The image of his father, and of the Saturnine father archetype,* weighed heavily upon him, casting him into depression. Sam's father was joyless,

---

*This archetype is described more fully on p. 130.

without pleasures in life, remote, and intolerant; he imposed his limitations upon Sam's mother, who was weak as a feminine counterforce. She had a quiet warmth, however, that may have accounted for Sam's sociability and restrained, but real, feeling. When Sam as a boy had worked at his father's business, his father had expected perfection and been harshly critical of Sam, who in turn criticized his father's lack of enterprise in the world and overly cautious way of doing business.

What happens when a man is failed by his father, and the father principle is represented by arid Saturn? It extinguishes personal warmth and a connection to the feminine, making cold ashes of the hearth at home. A father who is both harsh and frightened drives out a son's hope of good authority in himself and others. Like his father, he can have a problem exerting control in his use of power, and in daring to move among men and meet adversity in the world.

At the least, a son is left with a bleak legacy. He is likely to feel compassion for his mother, a fellow sufferer. He yearns for what is missing in his family. But a son often chooses not to identify with his mother in this situation, because he cannot afford to identify with "weakness." He can rarely forego the male prerogatives of power in his household; the opposite is too devastating to his self-image. So he does not follow the way of the heart, but with guilt follows the way of power, in secret alliance with his father as a model. He may be doubly bound to this way by both parents' ambition for him—that he be powerful for them in the world.

What brought Sam into therapy was falling in love with a woman who was his opposite: youthful, cuddly, frail, mysterious, volatile, and wild. As he groped to find his clumsily loving side and made efforts to curb his criticalness, cynicism, and dominance, she abruptly rejected him. It was as if he were suddenly cut open. He said that he sought therapy so as not to lose access to his emotions now that they were opened up. He wanted a different fate from his father's. He knew deep inside that this opening up to the feminine and Eros was the key for him, and he had the courage to stay open.

Our ensuing therapeutic work together nourished his emotional relatedness and he began to hope for a warm hearth in his life. Then he came to a juncture in his professional life where he dared to make a change; he experienced considerable anxiety as he left his well-established work for something risky, but possibly more rewarding. He used his assertiveness to work for him in therapy and in his life. He moved steadily ahead for a year, keeping alive the flame that had been ignited, and ventured further into his unconscious.

Sam had done "all the right things" long enough. The time had come for his opening up to dance, to song, to beauty in the outside world; and inside, to find what was truly meaningful to him. It was play—an aspect of the spirit of Pan—which would help him take the next step. He did his first sand world.

### THE PRINCE AND THE MONKEY

This sand world (Plate 2) not only gives a picture of Sam's inner world, but also shows how, in the course of the sandplay, he made

PLATE 2
The Prince and the Monkey.

a profound step forward. I will present his description of each part of the sand world in the sequence in which he created it. I will also include material from our overall therapy when it is relevant to understanding the figures. The first phase of his sand world went as follows:

> *I'm on the throne or seat. The mischievous monkey* [to left of throne] *mocks me, and plays tricks. Goading. Tries to get me off the chair. But the old man, pathetic, implores me to stay in the chair.*

*The throne.* Sam is at a decisive juncture in his life. The dynamic opposition is between staying in a high position or leaving it; between heeding conservative Saturn or the instincts.

This expresses a culmination of his growing awareness of the "prince" role with which he had identified all his life. Since he was very young his parents and relatives had recognized his outstanding capability; they told him time and again that they expected him to grow up to be "the mayor of the city." Indeed, when he began therapy at age 32 he had attained an apex of outer success—professionally, materially, and in terms of humanitarian contributions. However, it had been "too easy," he said. He felt restless, yet immobilized in not knowing what he wanted. It was as if he had inherited a title to an easily acquired kingdom, which then left him and his heroic side without a worthy quest of its own.

*The monkey.* In explaining the sand world, Sam said that the monkey was "fun-loving; doesn't have to work." His own life had been filled with hard work. I think the monkey represents natural instinct for mobility in the world that is carefree, joyful, quick-moving, and unself-conscious. But this monkey is not to be trusted. Afterward, I puzzled over why the monkey had such a critical, cynical manner, as if tempting him into dissolution. One reason might be that as a teenager he had been left free to roam the city streets, because his parents were in awe of his intelligence and his *chutzpah.* He could come and go as he pleased at home, ask for what he wanted, and bully his mother. I would guess that this experience of adolescent independence and parental abdication of authority made him feel suspicious about his "monkey" side. For he knew the doubtful benefits of the adolescent monkey's aggressive license, detachment from social restraint, and freedom to wander through the world without a guide. Sam had continued that pattern in still being self-sufficient in his life. He worked for himself and lived by himself. He tended to be too extraverted and too aggressive in relating to potential partners at work or home; and he also set too high standards for himself and others, then felt critical. Yet it seemed to me that he suffered from being alone, as he was gregarious by nature.

*The old man.* Sam had talked and dreamed a lot about "the old man" who seemed to be running his life underneath the surface of consciousness. He felt angry at his father's stern old-country authority, and on the other hand dismayed and betrayed by his father's weakness and lack of authority, evinced in his permissiveness and deference to himself, the son; for example, the father asked Sam to drive his car for him because Sam was a "better driver." Yet Sam had identified unconsciously with his father. Sam looked older than his years, and thought wistfully of retiring too. It was as if a gray cloud hung over him, draining him of his youth, making him pessimistic and tired, like an old man.

This sand world clarified two things that were important for Sam's therapy: (1) He had unconsciously accepted a strong mandate from his father to live out his ambition for him. Henceforth, Sam could perceive the "prince" aspect of his life, his old position of achieving for his father and relatives, within their narrow definitions of material success. (2) He discovered that he had compassion for his father. I think it is very important here that he called the old man "pathetic." By this time in therapy he had moved far enough away from identifying with his father as an archetype to see him as a person, and yet had moved closer in compassion. A stern and remote father who cannot make a personal bond with his son can be seen as an impersonal embodiment of collective norms, with all their power to possess; but the spell can be broken through fellow-feeling, and this is what Sam found it in his heart to do. One of the most important turning points in his therapeutic journey came later, when he visited his father in the hospital. His father

cried, and Sam touched him for the first time, and was moved. As
he tried to understand the feelings that had been opened up, he realized that when he and his father had touched before, it had been
in hurt and anger. That had been a strong unconscious bond all his
life, holding him down. This new bond of compassion released
him.

Sam's sandplay continued, and he explained the little painted
figure in the lower left corner.

*The imp watches over me to see what happens. Smirking, devilish. He
has ultimate wisdom of what goes on. He's permanent.*

*The imp.* This figure, as he describes it, sounds to me like an archetypal counterpart to the monkey, the animal trickster. It carries
a hint of Pan, and is in league with the monkey who also has detachment enough to mock the prince's self-importance. The imp
has godlike wisdom that probably comes from impiety and
knowledge of the profane. It represents the shadowy, demonic
side of the spiritual. I can imagine behind this figure the father's
lack of spirit, and the warning that to leave the sure path of the father's old ways is to face the danger of falling prey to disaster. On
the other hand, I sense in this figure a positive aspect. It seems to
me that the trickster, the clown, the jester, and the fool, had all
been neglected in Sam's life, and their gifts had almost been lost—
the laughter, the magic, the erotic, the absurd, and, most important, the transcendent. The imp could help restore these aspects by
his contempt for respectability, thus challenging the old order of
Saturn, and allowing the possibility of the flowing forth of the
new, masculine spirituality.

Where does this leave Sam? The sandplay sequence continued.
He explained:

*The shells are deep and full. They can receive, but they're cold.*

*The shells.* I think the shells express his relationship to the feminine; he feels cut off from its warmth and life-giving force. As
men under the Saturnine archetype often do, he usually chose suitable women companions whom he could respect—intelligent, de-
pendable, but unexciting. The shells in the sand world highlight

another quality of such women—their cool receptiveness. I see this kind of woman as a good listener, but mostly listening in a rational way, leaving a man essentially isolated. The shells reminded me of another form his feminine side (anima) took; he had a great love of beauty, especially art, and of the rapture it held for him.

Sam did not mention the *Krishna figure* between the shells and the throne. The fact that he did not mention it makes me realize now that it was probably an unconscious part of his psyche, beyond the reach of his conscious awareness. I think the figure represents a new healing potential, deep within himself, unconsciously moving him in his therapeutic journey.

The sandplay remained locked in conflict for a long time. Then, something happened. Sam laid three little figures in the sand in front of the throne.

*The little figures are me, off the throne. Helpless, stone, lacking vitality. Almost dead. They're like children.*

*The three children.* Sam had moved from his extraverted lofty heights to the opposite, an inert child-like state. This was the passive, helpless, immature, inner side of himself from which he had been cut off. He was daring now to explore the opposite polarity of his father's usual old man stance and had found dead children there. The old man casts sour looks at what is childlike in our nature. I think this shows the profound effect on a son of a father's fear and disdain of human weakness. At first a son rejects weakness and knows only strength, his father's and his own, so when he finally confronts weakness it looks very weak indeed. When he does so, however, he can then accept the softer feelings of warmth, spirit, and hope in his life. Later in therapy, Sam felt his vulnerability during a deep depression and anxiety. He had the courage to look his father in the eyes, and saw fear and sadness there. He realized that his father was a separate, ordinary person; and he did not have to carry his father's unconscious feelings for him anymore. He could take his own risks, in work and love.

After the fall from the throne and the appearance of the dead children, positive signs appeared in the sand world:

*The egg: comfortable, wholeness. A bird is over the egg. A hopeful sign. There's a connection between the two. The glass: strong, solid, luminescent clarity, roundness, layered, light-giving. The spiral shell is a gravity source. It works its way up* [the spiral]. *It's something to hold onto. A new process with color. Becomes an egg.*

*The egg.* Sam did not know what these symbols meant, but in contemplating them we can conjecture that the egg suggests his containment and contentment with life lived within parental expectations. He did bask in his parents' pride in his accomplishments. It is not a lizard egg, but a bird egg. And it is associated with a bird in flight, which I see as the possibility of the birth within him of an uplifting, soaring quality that he so much needed.

*The luminescent glass.* Along the same vein, the luminescent glass suggests the prospect of wholeness through consciousness and enlightenment of the spirit.

*The spiral seashell* is central to this cluster of objects. It is an unusual, delightfully colorful spiral, and I think it refers to an inner development of his sense of life-force, through feelings and love of beauty, which had been nurtured in therapy. It was "something to hold onto"; that is, even though he might feel anxious, he could feel security within himself, in trusting the healing factor in his inner development.


AFTERMATH

What happened immediately after the construction of this sand world attests to the profound and spontaneous breakthrough of the transcendent function when opposites have been brought to light, as they were in this sandplay. At the next session, Sam told me about a dream so powerful that he said it came with sharp pain:

*A golden throne in the sky. There's a glow around it, well lit up, in a dark sky. It wasn't me in the sky; it was God. Shining and powerful. I was glad to see it. Two shells pointed to the throne. They were at my level, but they pointed up. It was the path for me to get there. Then it faded. I didn't go now, but I had a path to get there. I felt like it was an answer to a prayer.*

I did not sense that he was inflated as he told the dream, but rather that he had a respectful feeling of placing worship where it was due. Years earlier he had belonged to an intellectual sect of the Jewish religion, then had dismissed religion from his life. The dream was a sudden and deep religious experience for him. In Jungian terms, it was the sudden gift of "knowing" the divine side of the Father archetype. He had let go of his presumption to the throne in order to take his rightful place in relation to it.

After the dream, as therapy unfolded, Sam seemed to undergo a basic reorientation in various parts of his life, which I now understand as the effect of his reconciliation with the Father archetype. He said that he knew now that he had to work, and it had to be meaningful work. He was learning to curb his aggression, and to admit his weaknesses, as well as his real need for others. In the subsequent year he began to consolidate three areas in his life: (1) The spiritual. He found a small synagogue with a warm, sincere rabbi and a sense of sharing among its community, a feeling rather than an intellectual relation to the Divine. (2) Work. He dared to move ahead in a new work venture, anxious at times but with newly found confidence that all would go well. (3) Love. He was more attracted to women with artistic or lively spirits.

He was well on his way to escaping from his father's fate. He had come a long way from what Neumann (1971) calls "patriarchal castration," the state in which the son's ego identifies with his personal father and his limitations (losing touch with inspiration and his own spiritual nature), or else identifies with the Father-god and is inflated (losing touch with his own earthly limitations).

> For the fathers' sons, the hero-bearing goddess is blotted out by the Terrible Father. They live entirely on the conscious plane and are incarcerated in a kind of spiritual uterus that never allows them to reach the fruitful feminine side of themselves, the creative unconscious. . . . The heroism that has been stifled in them manifests itself as sterile conservatism and a reactionary identification with the father, which lacks the living, dialectical struggle between the generations. (pp. 189-190)

# Case Study: Thomas

Thomas was in his 30s, and looked younger than his years. He had a youthful spirit, an engaging buoyant way of talking, and an unconscious that flowed over the riverbanks. His heart had been touched by the "mother-magic" of inspiration. He felt destined for the heights. But his father's conventional, unimaginative way of thinking had left its imprint—his fear of failing. More than that, he was left with his parents' definition of success, not his own. His main image of success was essentially performing for them to see him. He was predominantly introverted, and it seemed to me, as we began therapy, that his validation essentially needed to come from within, not from outside.

Thomas came from the heartland of the southwest hill country, where people eke out a living in an impoverished land, lacking opportunity in life beyond the rutted road of basic necessities and fundamentalism, sometimes lightened by the spirit of humor and song. Significant in his personal history was the fact that his mother had worked and sacrificed to put her brother through school, but she was the talented one, and her brother a wastrel. So she had made certain that she married a hard-working man who had a steady job. Thomas was their only child.

Thomas was very bright and talented, with a deep joy in his creations. His mother, however, had driven him to "market" his talents, and his father, as a matter of course, had always scoffed at his son's creations. Thomas needed to be brought down to plodding earth, but his father's scoffing directly attacked his core values and hurt his self-worth. He found it hard to respect his father, whom he saw as caught in conformity at work and conventionality at home. He hated to think of such a narrow track in life for himself.

Thomas came into therapy at loose ends, confused, and anxious. His primary reason for seeking therapy was related to the mother sphere: he had been turned down by a school, and it looked as if he was not talented enough to fulfill his mother's dreams. He had begun to wonder even if he wanted to work that hard, knowing how difficult it is to make a living in the arts. Yet he could hardly give up his lifelong dream. He felt torn apart.

In therapy, he weathered the crash to earth of his hopes, and in the process untangled the legacy from his mother—the tying together of creativity with approval and high ambition. He managed to retain his creative spirit while largely shaking it free from performing and materialism.

The second reason he came in was a jolting development in the father sphere. Set adrift from his life ambition in the mother sphere of creativity, he had delved into the father sphere. He had always been optimistic and quick, going from one job to another. He would start with enthusiasm, overwork, then feel disillusioned with each boss, and try the next. Then things changed. He had gone to work for a man who was all that his father was not: deeply philosophical, worldly-wise, a good teamworker with other men, and respectful of Thomas. Thomas, as a feeling type man, had intense longings for clarity and vision in the thinking sphere. Now at last he had a wonderful sense of belonging to a group of men, and they were in the heroic enterprise of developing thought for constructive uses. The very brightness of his new consciousness cast into dark shadow the narrow thinking of his background. He realized his alienation from and fear of his father, who was authoritarian and competitive about small things, and felt his own smallness in never being able to challenge him for fear of retaliation. It was also an inner battle, between his own old thinking and his new vision. However, the work, and hence the relationship with his supervisor, eventually came to an end.

Since Thomas was an intuitive feeling type, this connection to a personal father figure and the Father archetype had led him to high spiritual and philosophical heights. But it had also led him to the opposite—fantasies of aggression and coarse, dehumanized sexuality which at times intruded into consciousness. These shocked him deeply. Through time, in the course of therapy, he came to understand these fantasies as the dark side of his newly found spirit and instinct, split off earlier by his religious and home background; and he found channels for his newly found perspective and energy. Gradually, he again found relatively satisfying and challenging work and in the next years established his own household. He developed a very different and more individual (and satisfying) relationship to the woman he lived with than his parents had shared in their conventional home life.

Neumann (1971) talks about the kind of shift Thomas made when he changed from his father's kind of life at work and home.

> The monotonous sameness of fathers and sons is the rule in a stable culture. . . . The exception is the creative individual—the hero. . . . The "inner voice," the command of the transpersonal father or father archetype who wants the world to change, collides with the personal father who speaks for the old law. We know this conflict best from the Bible story of Jehovah's command to Abraham: "Get thee out of thy country, and from thy kindred, and from thy father's house, unto a land that I will show thee" (Genesis 12:1). (p. 178)

After three years of therapy, Thomas did the following sandplay drama. (I will present scenes in the sequence in which he created them.)

### THE DOME

First he shaped a mountain, then rows of boxes. He worked with frustrating carefulness to try to make the sand (a very loose element) into very smooth and straight boxes:

*A mountain. A city block, surrounded by the ocean. There's decay at the center.*

He erased it all, and then labored over one large box:

*It's a large outdoor movie theater screen.*

He destroyed the theater, and waited. Then he shaped a sphere with an opening:

*A cave, where early man stayed for a long time.*

He destroyed the cave, and began the last scene (see Plate 3). At first he made two domes with a connection between them. Then he said, "No, it's only one," and made one large dome.

PLATE 3
The Dome.

*It's rough (not smooth). There's a garden on the left. The pond nearby* [the dark spot in center background] *has fish. Not to eat. They're wild. The mountain doesn't have sheer cliffs like Mt. Everest. It's easier than that. You can climb it, like Mt. Tamalpais. A stream goes down the mountain side to the pond. There's a garden. The people are vegetarians. They get nourishment from nature, a fitting relation to nature. It's not like before, with concrete over the real stuff* [earth]. *Not like the church* [with its perfectionism that overlays human nature as it is]. *You can see the dome from the outside. But the most interesting thing is from the* inside. *Its glass windows look out to the dome of the sky.*

Thomas was deeply moved as he was doing this sand world, and I was profoundly moved watching him with his hands in the earth, shaping his worlds. He first labored to make the sand into smooth, perfect boxes, which seemed to me a representation of how society had tried to "work him over." He had tried hard to conform to the outer collective, but it had left decay in his inner core. The dictionary defines decay as a slow wasting away from soundness to decomposition. Thomas saw the decay in a city core, with its overly organized structure, cemented-over earth, and political corruption; that is, he saw decay in a projected, collective form. I saw it as a danger within him.

He did not know what the movie screen meant, but some thoughts came to my mind. Its being an *outdoor movie screen* suggests the *projection* (movie screen) of images within the context of *nature* (outdoors); that is, Thomas was playing out things at some distance so that he could see them anew. When he finished this part, and was leveling the overlarge theater, as he had leveled the city in the scene before, I had an intuition that it was his performing career that he was also sacrificing to start life afresh.

We both saw the next cave scene, a return to earliest man and his natural shelter, as his return to the basic origins, or the materials to rebuild society (his inner structure).

In contrast to his cramped and careful work in the previous scenes, he sculpted the final scene with free, sure movements of his hands and left it "rough," reminding me of the way a painter uses broad brush strokes. Afterwards, we talked back and forth about the last scene in much the same spirit. It emerged that the people had a good relation to "raw nature," and that he too needed to go back to the instincts—sex and aggression, in their raw, natural form, to find his own relation to them. He had a special feeling about the dome, which looks to me like a self symbol, a human within the context of a wider firmament.

He was deeply moved by this sand world in subsequent weeks. In the next therapy session, he had reached further understanding of the dome:

> *I imagine a naked man in the nature scene. Where could I put him? Inside the dome, where he has its protection. I feel as if I myself am looking out of the dome. The whole sandtray is a proper stand in relation to nature—a greater nature and point of view.*

What happened in the sandplay was also manifested in his life and how he saw its deeper purpose. During the session he related how he had successfully persuaded everyone where he worked to let him take on a new project. The project held great passion and meaning for him. It was a vast undertaking, and challenged his creativity. It was starting at the beginning and bringing order out of chaos, through great concentration and sustained effort. These are the heroic ego tasks required for a man to prove himself. But it seemed more than that, too. The crux of the passion and meaning that it held for him was the relationship between the overall structure and the smaller structures underneath. It was important that the overall structure be sound enough so that the smaller structures, while autonomous, could fit into the overall one "and never mess it up." I see this as his passionate concern that the ego be subordinate to a higher organizing principle, ultimately the self—as depicted in the sand world, the dome, and its relationship to the firmament.

# Mistakes, Exceptions,
# and Special Considerations

By trial and error through the years, I have stumbled across some useful principles about sandplay. I suppose it is when we stub our toes that we notice basic things we might have otherwise overlooked, and see them more clearly.

### THE THERAPEUTIC CONTEXT OF THE SANDPLAY PROCESS

I have made some mistakes that show how important it is for a therapist to maintain a secure atmosphere, a therapeutic container for the healing process, the *temenos* that is so important in Jungian analysis.

One day a friend expressed interest in doing a sand world. He was a cold, self-sufficient man in his 40s. I introduced him to the sandtray, and sat nearby in silence. Shortly after he began I left the

room to get a pitcher of water for him to use in the sandtray, and
to stop by the bathroom. (I had had a small intuition that I should
not leave, but overruled it.) I had been gone only a few moments
before I resumed my place at his side. However, after the sandplay
he told me that it had been deeply disruptive to him. Here was a
self-sufficient man with a strong ego. But he had "let go" to his
unconscious because he had trusted me to be there with my ego,
and my supportive presence. This small incident made me realize
the vital importance of the therapist's presence in maintaining safe
and intact the therapeutic "container."

I made a similar error with another person. The patient (referred
by a mutual friend) was an experienced therapist himself, and had
had years of various kinds of therapy. He wanted to do a sand
world during our first session, and I agreed. Then I watched
transfixed with awe and horror as he did a sand world of an innermost, fragile, undifferentiated, and deep part of himself, threatened by an enormous demonic figure. He put rows and rows of
little stones around the center, to protect and contain it in the sandtray. Too much had burst forth, too soon. He did not come back
to a second session. I do not recall any other time that a patient has
done a sandtray without being in analysis with me for some time.
Why did I allow this? Because of the nature of the referral (a mutual friend), the patient's air of autonomy and toughness, and the fact
that he was a therapist, I had slipped into the patient's unconscious
casualness about the therapeutic container. I had not taken charge.
I had let the patient recklessly plunge into the unconscious without
assessing his ego defenses, or establishing our relationship and its
protection. Instead of the presence of the healing factor, we got a
demon.

On the other hand, I take exception to the fear I have heard expressed that the sandplay process is so powerful that it can be risky
for certain patients, should be done only in the presence of a therapist, and then only later in therapy. I have done sand worlds on my
own for years: so have friends and colleagues. On occasion, if I
have a cold for day after day, I might do a sand world. When I am

at the beach I sometimes draw a circle in the sand,* and gather my objects from the beach.

I think there is a general fear of all forms of active imagination—painting, fantasy, clay, sandplay. They are potent, and taboos and superstitions develop around any mishap. I do not want to be misunderstood, and add to the taboos! I am *not* saying that therapists should never leave the room; or should never allow sandplay during the first session. I would rather emphasize that a therapist's choices about the nature and timing of sandplay need a balance of conscious and unconscious processes in the decision-making itself.

In the case above, in which I left the room, I had let my practical ego overrule my unconscious intuition that I should stay. My unconscious knew that the patient needed to keep the *continuity* of whatever container had been set up, just as, when I construct a sand world on my own, I know that I have to provide my own structure: an undisturbed atmosphere to let the unconscious flow, my own ego defenses, and most important, the presence of the healing factor.

My own way of being introduced to sandplay worked well for me. I had been in therapy for many years when I asked my analyst about sandplay. Being practical, I suggested doing sand worlds on my own. She wisely suggested that she first introduce me to the sandtray in her office, and we did several worlds together. Then, when I did them on my own, I had her presence with me. I had by then absorbed within myself an appropriate attitude from hearing her directions, and the healing factor was constellated. I took pictures and brought them to her so that the sandplay was kept within the circle of the therapy.

Another example illustrates the importance of the therapeutic relationship, and a patient's relationship to the healing spirit. Some

---

*Incidentally, I naturally gravitate to a circle, a feminine container, not the traditional rectangle, and would have a round sandtray in my office if it were feasible!

years ago, a colleague referred a patient to me specifically for sand-play therapy. She had been seeing him for years. He wanted to do sandplay therapy, and since she did not have a sandtray he was to do a weekly sand world with me and take a picture of it back to her for discussion in their regular sessions. It sounded plausible then (although it does not now). It turned out to be a fiasco. I was aware of the awkwardness of the situation, and our need to estab-lish some relationship between us, but viewed in retrospect, it was mere tokenism. He spent several sessions working in the sandtray, as well as talking a little, before and after. What is of interest for us here is what happened—or rather, did *not* happen—in the sandplay therapy. The patient worked in the sandtray, with archetypal im-ages and animals, but it seemed flat to me. He was going through the motions, but nothing happened; we both realized it and he quit working with me.

At first I thought it was because we did not have enough of a feeling relationship between us, and it was partly that. But it was more. The transcendent function was missing in this sandplay process. He had been sent to me because something was lacking at that stage of his therapy work. As his therapist said, "He works hard, but it is as if the gears don't mesh right now in therapy. I thought that something might happen if he could play." But the same thing occurred in sandplay. Somehow, we all unconsciously fell into thinking that the experience itself might be enough. And sometimes the experience does set something in motion; one can only wait and see if the magic of the third factor comes in. But in that case we had stacked the decks against ourselves. It was not that a person cannot have two therapists; I have seen that work very well. But that in our emphasis on a technique, we had over-looked the importance of our role as healers within the therapeutic relationship, in constellating the transcendent function. The pa-tient did a prognostic sand world, but it was a scattering of ob-jects, without a path; in another sand world he indicated opposites in a desultory way, but each remained on its own side of the tray; on another occasion he put out the golden throne toppled over backward, half-buried in the sand. That is, his world embodied no stance, no presence, but only experience for its own sake. We had not validated his "I" having the experience; we had not given it its proper importance ourselves.

In contrast is the case of another patient who was going through an agitated depression, and had a precarious hold over his outpouring of affect. He felt deeply drawn to a Buddha figure on my sandplay shelves. I do not ordinarily lend or give away sandplay figures, but he asked for it, and I gave it to him for a few weeks while he needed it. Several weeks later, he brought it back. It had been very helpful to him as a "transitional object," as if he were taking the therapeutic healing spirit home with him until the inner figure became constellated within himself.

### GENERAL CONSIDERATIONS

There are other considerations regarding the ego and the healing factor that I have found important to keep in mind. If a person's ego is not strong enough, it seems to me that all that happens when he engages in active imagination, especially if he is alone, is that the unconscious merely overflows. Patients often report that they have fantasies (usually more passive than active) on their own, and of course in those circumstances the therapist has little responsibility or control. It is a different story, though, if we as therapists initiate an active imagination experience such as sandplay: whether patients have a weak ego or are setting aside a strong ego, they trust us to decide whether the experience will be *therapeutic*. That is, we therapists need to assess whether it will result in a balance of conscious and unconscious, without the unconscious overwhelming the ego or vice versa, and whether there is a possibility that the healing factor will emerge. Sometimes one takes a calculated risk, and both therapist and patient share that risk, as with the patient I mentioned earlier who worked through his suicidal impulses. Sometimes the therapist needs to say "No," just as I discourage some patients from doing active or passive fantasies at home when I see that the activity will be counter-productive because the unconscious will overwhelm the patient with affect or images. I try to correct the mistaken idea patients sometimes have that in terms of the unconscious flow the *more* there is the better. That is true only in balanced relation to conscious control and the ability to resolve the experience—i.e., in relation to the transcendent function.

TYPOLOGICAL CONSIDERATIONS

In introducing sandplay to patients, the analyst needs to be sensitive to the needs of different psychological types.

The extraverted sensation type (outgoing and concrete) usually finds that it is easy to give outer form to his inner world in sandplay. He may want to share his enthusiasm about this discovery by pointing out all the objects he has used—probably a great array of them. This is easy for him, but can remain somewhat empty as an experience. He needs to complement this by becoming aware of the opposite—the introverted intuitive (inner and abstract). That is a harder task for patient and analyst—to look behind the forms in all their repetitive detail, down the inner road to the general archetypes. The patient needs to know what gives the forms their substance.

One avenue for the analyst is to inquire how the objects *move* the patient. I may ask the extraverted sensation type what is most important to him about the whole sand world (a feeling intuitive task). For instance, "What do you like about it?" or "What are the relationships between objects?" Strong affect toward certain images might lead such a patient to be able to name the archetype. For instance, "feeling overwhelmed" is likely to mean the Great Mother; allurement or mystery, the anima. I may ask the patient to ponder an overall title for the sand world (an intuitive-thinking task). Sometimes I tentatively suggest a general thought about the meaning of the sand world, and this can be very helpful to the extraverted sensation type in understanding his inner state.

It is different for the therapist working with an introverted intuitive person. One needs to be sensitive to the introverted intuitive's richness of inner images, but also to the frustration accompanying the sand world because giving the images outer form does not do them justice. Yet the patient needs to give them outer reality and I wait for anything he might want to say. I am careful not to refer to any object by presuming that I know what it is. What looks like a green parrot to me might mean something very different to the patient! I am careful about interpreting, and merely ask if he wants to say anything about the experience or what is happening in the sandplay. If the patient is willing, I may express an interest in detail, and he may wish to go on from there. I am careful about judgments or interpretations and usually inquire in the feminine spirit of "walking around" the sand world as in dream amplification.

CONCLUSION

I have used the term "Saturnine" several times in this paper, and I think it is worth saying a little more about this concept in conclusion, because to my mind the spirit of Saturn weighs heavily on men in western society.

According to the myth, the god Saturn had to kill his father Uranus in order to be born, and thereafter eternally to devour his own children in order to stay in power, until at last he in turn was slain and supplanted by his own son, Jupiter.

The archetype of Saturn stands for order and control, the intellect and consciousness, awareness of consequences and the melancholy spirit. Control, measurement, structure, limitation are prominent features in the psyche of Saturnine man. His negative side is pessimism, overcautiousness, self-doubt, cold aloofness, lack of instinctual desires or Eros, intolerance, and rigidity. On the more positive side is self-determination, self-examination, high standards for himself and others, ethical and moral consciousness, carefulness, and responsibility.

Western society is biased heavily toward consciousness, and hence toward Saturnine values. Men are raised to work hard, and shaped to fit businesses, bureaucracies, and life-styles that are generally conservative and rule-bound. It is hard for a man who identifies with Saturn and is caught in "success," and for his opposite, the puer (or Fool) who is constantly devalued by Saturnine society. Sam is a good example of the first, weighed down by depression and success, not knowing how to let the "stone children" in his sandtray come alive. And Thomas illustrates the opposite, the artistic spirit, whose parents' expectations and judgments about failure or success constantly aimed to shape him into the "perfect boxes" in his sandtray.

Clinically speaking, if we as therapists are to reach thinking-type Saturnine men especially, and help them find their way to what is lost, I believe we need to align ourselves with the opposite and complementary spirit—the feminine, the feeling, the childlike: the spirit of play. Hence the enormous potential, for ourselves and our male patients, of sandplay, the activity which offers them license with restraint, freedom within structure, fantasy in safety, spontaneity allied with form and meaning.

We and our patients can do no better than remember and rejoice in the experience of Jung himself (1965), for whom at a time of adult crisis "it was a painfully humiliating experience to realize that there was nothing to be done except play childish games." Sustained only by "the inner certainty that [he] was on the way to discovering [his] own myth," Jung persisted in his play, incorporated playing into his life, and affirmed, "Each such experience proved to be a *rite d'entrée* for the ideas and works that followed hard upon it" (pp. 174-175).

# A Woman's Individuation Through Sandplay

KATHERINE BRADWAY

A question sometimes asked about sandplay is whether it only reflects the place one has reached in one's individuation, or whether it truly brings about the individuation. Is the creating of a sand world the therapy itself? I think it both effects and reflects: the creative process is always therapeutic, and the product of the process may be representative of the stage of one's development.

Before presenting the sandplay journey of Ida, which I believe illustrates the individuation process through sandplay, I want to offer a few comments about my use of the method. Because there are multiple variations in the practice of therapists who use sandplay, no one can recommend a set procedure, but I think the sharing of individual observations and experiences is of value.

The technique is referred to by the terms sandtray, sandplay and sand world; each term serves a different function in describing the process. Sandtray refers to the vehicle, sandplay to the activity, and sand world to the product. Within a tray of sand, in the serious spirit of play, you make a world. This private place, the sandtray, is provided by your therapist who remains nearby but apart. The open space is large enough to hold a segment of your inner world, but has firm boundaries around the edges to contain it. You feel free but protected.

In specifying the dimensions for my sandtrays, I meticulously followed those appearing in the English translation of Dora Kalff's book of sandplay: 19½ × 28½ × 3 inches, only to discover later that there was a discrepancy between the first dimension and the dimensions of Kalff's own sandtrays, due apparently to an error in the "translation" of centimeters into inches! As Clare Thompson* has already emphasized, however, the outer details are of minimal importance compared with what the process is all about.

The positioning of the sandtrays and objects to be used in them varies with different therapists. My sandtrays—one dry, one damp—are at counter height and stationary, with shelves of objects above the trays and on the sides, within easy reach as one stands at the tray. A high stool is provided if one wishes to sit down, but most persons stand until the world is completed. The absence of a standard collection of objects for use in the tray has an advantage in that the uniqueness of each therapist's collection provides for the interaction with something personally connected with—or an extension of—the therapist, and therefore the process remains within the framework of the transference.

Some clients shun plastic miniatures and choose instead those made of wood, stone, metal, clay. There is often a particular appreciation of shells, dried leaves, fruit pits (smooth avocado pit; rough "flame-like" peach pit), driftwood, sea-washed stones, dark lava pieces. The floor of the tray is painted blue so that pools and streams can be easily represented by clearing sand away from the bottom. The water I provide for additional watering of the damp sandtrays is in a squeezable spray bottle. Persons may sometimes use no objects, preferring to mold the sand with their hands and form furrows and designs with their fingers.

Therapists develop their own ways of introducing people to the sandtray. When I was studying with Frau Kalff, I adopted her invitation to the client to "Look over the shelves until you find something that speaks to you and put it in the tray and then add to it as you wish." I like this, but I don't always use it. I have no set in-

---

*Clare Thompson, "Variations on a Theme by Lowenfeld," this volume p. 5.

structions. They evolve out of the circumstances. At the first appointment I show the client what I call the "nonverbal room" because it has not only the sandplay setup, but also paints and clay and colored tissues. I explain that the time will come when he or she may want to come here and work with some of this material. Later, either the client or I will recognize that the time is right and we go to this room. At this point I will show the sandplay material, and say that world makers may use any objects or miniatures they choose, or if they prefer, use none. I show that the floor of the tray is blue and I may sift some of the sand through my own fingers just to be getting the feel of it myself.

Some clients are initially self-conscious, but the material usually takes over and many people welcome the departure from the more rational approach of verbal communication. I have found sandplay particularly useful when clients are either blocked in verbal expression or caught up in a stream of oververbalization.

Occasionally a person comes to me anticipating working with the sandtray and wants to use it at the first session. I think it is better to wait until a secure *temenos* has been established within the therapeutic relationship.    As the client works in the sandtray, I sit out of view and record the order of placement and the location of objects. The latter helps me identify objects in the pictures that I take later. To aid in noting location, I have marked the edges of the trays into five divisions down the sides, which I think of as A, B, C, D, E; and seven divisions across the top, which I think of as 1 through 7. In my notes, I can record, for example, "B-7 Totem pole" or "E-6 crying baby."

Interaction during the sandplay is usually minimal. Since comments about what the client is doing may be disruptive, I avoid them. The extent of verbal exchange about the sand world after it is completed varies. I find that if I ask a few questions to help me understand what is happening in the initial couple of scenes, the client tends to develop a pattern of completing a scene and then volunteering some explanatory remarks. My commenting on the reappearance of a particular object or of a particular theme usually elicits additional remarks from the client. But often there is a mutual recognition that the completed scene is a full expression in itself, and there is an understanding silence.

I think it is important that sand worlds are left intact and not dismantled until after the clients have left, so that they can more easily carry with them the image of what they have produced. Of each sand world I take both a color slide, which I can later project upon a screen, and an instant print. The prints stay in the client's folder for mutual reference and are offered to him or her to keep when therapy is terminated.

After a series of five to ten sand worlds, or whenever there is a sense of coming to the end of a phase, we study the projected slides or prints of the series together, making connections between the scenes, and then between the progression of scenes and other aspects of psychological development. New insights may emerge or old ones be consolidated.

The making of a world and talking about it seldom takes up more than half of an hour session, so that the more traditional verbal therapy is not excluded. What the sandplay method does is to provide a protected space where the inner process can work more freely than in verbal interchanges, and where the circumstances are conducive to a suspension of the ego-censor and to a comfortable trusting of one's fantasies. Unlike the recounting of dreams, there is no "third party" go-between. The scene is there, just as it occurred.

I find that clients use the sandplay material in their own individual ways. Children are apt to make a "movie" rather than a single scene, and often want to make more than one scene by using both the damp and dry sandtrays. Adults may change the position of some of the objects, but they seldom act out a drama. A sequence of worlds across several sessions, however, frequently reflects an underlying story. Sometimes the repetition of a scene, with only minor variations, plays a prominent role (as Ida's story demonstrates). Some people have a story in mind when they start to make a sand world; it may even be a segment of a dream. For others the scene in the sandtray unfolds without their being aware of what is coming next; this kind of sand world we regard as having more unconscious content or involvement than a scene that is premeditated. Margaret Lowenfeld (1979, p. 35) differentiates between realistic and nonrealistic or symbolic features of sand worlds: symbolic features which are spontaneous and not contrived indicate engagement of the unconscious.

Karen Signell* hypothesizes that women analysts use sandtrays more with women clients than they do with men; my experience bears this out only to the extent that I see more women than men. Over the last five years, however, whereas only 80 percent of the women I have seen in therapy have used the sandtray, all of my male clients have used it, and with an average frequency at least as high as for women. As for differences in male and female worlds, I have observed a tendency for men to make more central mounds than women, and for women to make more central pools than men, but this is only a tendency and has many exceptions. For the woman whose material is now to be presented, the central pool played a most prominent role, but a few central mounds also appeared in her sand worlds.

# Ida

To illustrate how the individuation process takes place in sandplay, I am going to present the sandplay work of a 40-year-old woman whom we will call Ida.**

Ida was the kind of woman who wanted to understand with her intellect. She was a bright, introverted, intuitive woman whose feeling function was basically superior to her thinking function; but she had lived under the domination of rationality for so long

---

*Karen Signell, "The Use of Sandplay with Men," this volume p. 101.

**I want to express my deep appreciation to Dora Kalff, who saw the pictures of many of Ida's sandplay scenes, and made useful suggestions as well as pointing out symbolic meanings of some of the objects.

PLATE I
Sand world 1.

that she had grown to believe that masculine logic was superior to feminine eros, and thinking and reason superior to feeling and instincts. She felt that she had to use her intellect to "hold things together." By the time she was introduced to sandplay, nearly two years after beginning therapy with me, she had arrived at the point of recognizing her conflict between habitual dependency on patriarchal authority on the one hand, and appreciation for natural instinct on the other. In the next two years, in her 90 sessions with me Ida made 70 sandplay worlds. Typically she made a sand world in the first half of a session and we talked in the last half. As will become clear later, our post-sandplay interchanges in the first 44 sandplay sessions included talking about her sand world; but the 45th sand world marked a change in the course of her therapy, and few or no references were made to her subsequent productions. Since I do not generally take notes other than those related to the sandplay, I am limited in correlative data between each sand world and what was taking place in her life at the time she made it. But the point I think valuable to make is contained in the sequence of sandplay worlds and the general course of her illness. The first 44 sand worlds furnish a background, but it is the sequence of the last 26 worlds on which I wish to concentrate. I think this sequence shows in its minute changes the actual process of individuation.

Ida's initial sandplay world (Plate 1) depicts her primary conflict and anticipates a resolution. The animals in the left upper corner (elephant, cow, mare, and colt) represent her instinctual or natural or feminine side. The police at left center and lower left side (policeman standing with hand raised; policeman on motorcycle) represent patriarchal authority. Ida volunteered, "Law stops growth; I like the instinctual."

Ida identified herself with the diving girl right of center and indicated that she was going to go through the tunnel (the tunnel hole in the mound of sand to the lower right of the tray does not show clearly in this picture). The woman on the horse and the man on the bicycle are also headed toward the tunnel. It is as if Ida has turned her back on the conflict represented on the left side of the tray and is ready to submit to another direction, take a different course, find a third way. This suggests the operation of the transcendent function. The bicycle-riding man and horse-riding woman represent masculine and feminine parts of herself that are to accompany her on this journey.

Ida made no reference to the Indian grouping in the top right corner: a teepee with a chief, a squaw with a baby, a totem pole; and yet this is on the side to which she is headed. What could this segment of the scene represent? In retrospect I realized that Native American culture exemplifies a deeply ingrained, dual respect for both authority and instinct. So the upper right is the goal of an integration which would resolve the conflict. Ida's placement of figures on the left and in the center of this sandtray is probably on a conscious level. The fact that she did not refer to the Indian grouping suggests that this resolution is not conscious. It will be noted that in both top corners motherhood is portrayed. Ida was able to maintain a mutually supportive relationship with her three teenage children.

Ida's next 28 sand worlds over the next 11 months were dominated by a conscious struggle to extricate herself from the bondage to patriarchal authority that was linked with her idealization of her father, her husband, and her minister. She wanted to grow. Her reading in Jungian psychology was translated into some of her sand worlds. For example, one scene depicted four levels of consciousness; another showed the four psychological functions in their negative-positive and male-female manifestations. Some concentrated on masculine aspects of the psyche; others on female aspects. Several represented conscious hostility and vulnerability in her relationship with her husband. After completing each sand world Ida usually volunteered a description of what was going on and what each scene meant. There were no haphazard arrangements of figures. All of the items she placed in the tray played a part in a unified, often geometrical, whole.

In her outer life, Ida was trying to cope with an unhappy marriage, the critical illnesses of both parents, and guilt feelings about all three. Ida's anxiety fluctuated, but was always intensified when she had any gynecological symptoms requiring medical attention. Her initial entrance into therapy with another analyst had been after a psychotic break which followed a D&C. At the time I began seeing Ida, her gynecologist was trying to postpone further surgery until Ida's anxiety in that area could be diminished and her inner resources sufficiently strengthened to withstand what she perceived as being robbed of her femininity. Ida was working hard in therapy; she made a clay torso figure at home to use in the sand-tray as a representation of herself; she brought in dreams, drawings, poems, her diary. She took correspondence courses in psychology and writing so that she could write her own story; she took a class in sculpting. Each creative activity revealed her innate talents. She was highly commended for her essays and stories in her writing course and won a prize for one of her first pieces of sculpture. She read avidly in her eagerness to understand psychology and tried to apply what she was learning to break through a net of confusion regarding ideals and reality, masculine and feminine, sex and religion. In many sessions she bombarded me with questions, both general and personal, in all of these areas.

Despite all of Ida's dedication to her task, when her gynecologist felt it necessary to advise her that she might need further surgery in the near future, she suffered a second psychotic episode. But gains had been made. This episode was brought under control by medication and more frequent therapy sessions; hospitalization was not required.

At the time of the onset of the psychotic episode, Ida's sand worlds mirrored her increasing disturbance. In her 30th sandplay session, Ida had used the sandtray to portray her homicidal and suicidal fantasies by burying herself and her husband in the sand. Two sessions later she came in with intensified anxiety, expressed her distress at having "done such a thing" and hastened to unbury the figures by producing sand world 32, shown in Plate 2.

PLATE 2
Sand world 32.

The shadows behind the two figures at right center are from the indentations left after Ida had raised the figures up out of the sand. Since the world in which she had initially buried them had been dismantled, she reburied them, permitting her to go through the process of unburying them. This is one of the kinds of healing experiences that is offered by sandplay: it is more actual than either mental imagery or verbal expression, but avoids the risks of acting out in a real way. The figures on either side of her husband and herself represent their three children and me; the six figures on the left of the tray were described as "fictional or fantasy" figures. It was at this session that Ida reported to me what her gynecologist had told her of the possibility of impending surgery .

For the next three months Ida represented herself in varying roles and situations in the sandtray. She used the king and queen figures for the first time. She placed them in the center at three consecutive sessions and after using other themes for two sessions returned to the king and queen for one more session. I now feel that she was attempting to regain stability and control by representing a version of the royal conjunctio. She was trying desperately to think herself out of the dreaded place of psychotic disturbance.

Then one day Ida came in and put a single figure representing herself in the center of the tray—all alone. This did not appear to be a gesture of feeling abandoned or of giving up, but one of strength—the strength associated with being able to confront the fact of aloneness. In the session after bringing herself and husband back to life, Ida had placed figures representing herself and me alone in the sandtray. But this time she was all alone. This 45th session marked the turning point in her sandplay work and in the course of her illness. At the next session she came in saying she felt better; she was better. The psychotic episode was over.

At the 46th session Ida made the first of many centered pools (Plate 3). In this first one there is a stream into the pool from the bottom left corner, represented by clearing the sand away from the blue floor of the tray. A canoe in the pool holds two Indians. In the upper left corner Ida placed a tree, and the teepee and the Indian squaw with baby that had appeared in her initial sand world (Plate 1). Contrary to her practice with all her sand worlds prior to the one of herself alone, she volunteered no comments after mak-

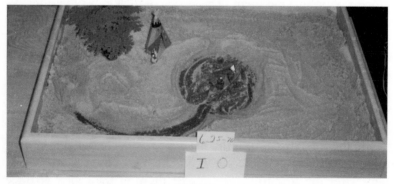

PLATE 3
Sand world 46.

PLATE 4
Sand world 48.

ing this one and I asked for none. It would seem, however, that the water coming from the lower left corner portrays energy coming to a centered inner place from the unconscious. It is a common phenomenon in the experience of both art therapists and sandplay therapists that left hand and lower parts of the picture or sand scene tend to represent the unconscious, whereas the right hand and upper parts represent the conscious. While not invariably true, this is sometimes a helpful guideline.

It is significant that the segment of Ida's initial tray that suggested a resolution to her conflict was peopled by Indians, and that the 46th world, which ushers in a new phase of her individuation process, is also peopled by Indians. None of the intervening 44 worlds included Indians. There appears to be a link between the initial world and this one made 15 months later. The sand world at the 47th session was similar to the 46th world; there were Indians in a canoe in a stream that connected the lower left with a central pool. But this time Ida added a piece of driftwood that looks like a huge rock when placed in the sandtray. This driftwood appeared in the next 20 sand worlds. In retrospect I think it provided a kind of solidness for her.

Animals appeared in the 48th sand world, and for the first time there were no humans. This world (Plate 4) conforms to what Kalff (1971, p. 24), referring to its appearance in children's sandtrays, calls the animal-vegetative stage or initial stage of ego development. I think that this apparent regression in Ida's case to an earlier stage of development coincides with her release from trying to reason things out. She is now able to let something happen without consciously willing it.* Again Ida made no comments, and rarely did so for the remaining 22 sand worlds.

It would be difficult to overemphasize the contrast between the sand worlds preceding and following the world-of-herself-alone. It was a truly significant turning point. She had left the intellectual stance and the psyche had taken over. A centering inner process had been activated, and she had stopped trying to make everything have a rational meaning. Perhaps by following the variations in these latter worlds we can sense her individuation process.

In the 49th sand world Ida abandoned the animals she had used in the 48th world and returned to showing humans. In addition to re-using the Indians-in-a-canoe from worlds 46 and 47, she used the diving girl, who had appeared in the initial world and infrequently since, but was to appear in most of her remaining worlds. She also used a girl lying on her stomach and a boy sitting near the girl, who were to reappear in the next 20 sand worlds. She usually placed them on top of the driftwood "rock." They may have represented parts of herself observing from a solidly secure place. At one point she commented, "It's like they are looking at a myth." We will recall that the feminine (woman on horse) and the masculine (man on bicycle) were shown in the initial sand world as accompanying the figure of the diving girl with whom Ida identified herself at the start of her journey through the tunnel. This confirms my earlier suggestion of a link between this final sequence of sand worlds and her initial world. It is as if Ida, or parts of herself, had gone through the tunnel to another space. Also in this 49th sand world Ida for the first time used a bridge over water. The bridge was placed over a channel which connected two bodies of

---

*Her world 48 can be compared with Plate 1 in my paper "Developmental Stages in Children's Sand Worlds," this volume p. 94.

water, so connections were shown between water masses as well as between land masses. Connections such as bridges and channels can represent the possibility, or the realization, of connecting links between parts of one's self. Perhaps the connections between land masses parallel connections between more conscious parts of one's self, and those between water masses connections between the less conscious parts of one's self.

Sand world 50 had a large mound of sand, rather than a pool, in its center, and thus anticipated two of the final worlds (68 and 69, Plates 10 and 11). This first mound was surrounded by water—a "mountain island" perhaps, like a self symbol rising from the unconscious. An Oriental ship replaced the Indian canoe as a water vehicle. The man and woman couple that Ida had unburied on world 32 and used once since were included here, probably in reference to her married self as compared with the more individual self, represented by the diving girl who continues to appear throughout these worlds. She also placed six trees in the scene. One or more trees, the symbol of growth, of life, appeared in each of the 25 worlds following the world-of-herself-alone. This was in marked contrast to the earlier worlds in which trees were the exception rather than the rule. In fact, in those earlier worlds so dominated by the intellect, symbols of any kind were infrequent. When they were used, it seemed to be in a studied, conscious manner.

In world 51 Ida again made a central pool, which was thereafter to form the center of all her worlds until the final three. At session 51 she brought some glue from home to mend the Oriental ship, having noticed it was broken when she had used it in her preceding world. The act of mending the ship seemed to coincide with the mending of her psyche, or perhaps signified repairing of the vehicle for her journey. A couple of sessions later she drove to my office by herself; it was the first time she had been able to come alone in many weeks.

Although most of the content of her sand worlds remained the same, an important addition appeared in world 52: treasures. Ida placed pieces of turquoise and three small colored spheres next to

PLATE 5
Sand world 53.

stones and a tree on the left center of the tray. On my inquiry, she identified the turquoise as treasure and said the diving girl on the right side was going to get it.

In world 53 (Plate 5) the turquoise and glass spheres are placed around the diving girl, who has been moved from the right side, where she had been appearing, to the left side, where the drift-wood with the sitting boy and lying-down girl have also been placed. I commented "She got over there," to which Ida replied, "Yes, I don't know what it is supposed to mean, but I felt like putting her there," thus demonstrating, perhaps, the primacy of feeling over thinking. This world is also the first since the 48th (shown in Plate 4) to include animals: here a cow and bull beside a tree. And it also marks the final appearance of the Oriental ship.

Worlds 54 and 55 were similar to 53 except for the omission of the Oriental ship and the treasures, and the inclusion of the man-woman couple. At the second of these sessions Ida remarked "I'm in a rut—doing the same thing."

In world 56 (Plate 6) the treasures return (they were to be a permanent feature until the final world). In 56 they are placed as before close to the diving girl. A new addition appears: a red raft in the center of the pool. From Indian canoe to Oriental ship to red

PLATE 6
Sand world 56.

raft. The raft would seem to have a double symbolic value: it is a means of keeping one above the water rather than diving into it, that is avoiding the risk of being lost in the unconscious; and its redness is a way of representing or holding onto the ever stronger feeling function. Moreover, on a raft one is nearer the water, almost a part of it, not enclosed from it as one is on a ship. Note also that beside a tree on the right side a calf has been added to the cow and bull, making a family. This is the first time that an animal family with both parents has been shown. The redness of the raft and the family relatedness of the animals reinforce one another in pointing to a more secure feeling function. The Japanese geisha appears for the third time in this series (she had appeared previously in 51 and 55). On one of her earlier appearances, Ida had commented that the geisha represented feminine mystery. She made no comments now. The thatched house had also appeared intermittently in previous worlds; houses are perceived as feminine symbols. And the boy and girl on the solid driftwood continue to look down onto the whole scene.

The following world (57) retained the animal parent and child but changed it from cow and calf to mare and colt—perhaps representing a transition from a complacent to a more spirited nurtur-

ing feeling. The man and woman couple that always stood together previously were here separated: the woman was joined in
the upper right of the tray by a bride, a milkmaid, and a witch,
representing three other aspects of the feminine; the man was
joined on the lower right by a knight on horseback. After the feeling function and the feminine are secure, a strong animus can appear. In this world, the two that preceded it, and several that followed it, the left side remained nearly identical, whereas the right
side changed.

The geisha ("feminine mystery") reappeared in world 58 and
continued to appear on the right side, rising from bottom to center
to top, until the last world. The red raft was now beached on the
shore. It had done its work and was not included again. For the
first time shells appeared, symbol of the feminine principle, along
with a well, symbol of access to nourishment from the unconscious. A cottage with a car in front of it indicated juxtaposition of
feminine and masculine.

The next four worlds were near duplications of 58 except for the
omission of the raft, the shells and the well. The knight on horseback, who first appeared in 57, was replaced in world 61 by two
black horses, which appeared in every world thereafter. After
completing 60, Ida made one of her rare comments: "The left is
contemplation; the right is the ideal and primitive and mystic,
and—I don't know." And after world 62 she said, "The left seems
inner, real, stable. The right, or outer, is changing." It was as if she
had observed this as a trend in her worlds rather than that she had
consciously tried to make them this way. She seemed to have a
growing recognition that something important was taking place
that did not require her conscious judgment or decision. Again,
she was letting something happen.

Sand world 63 included a dog and a cat on a stone jutting out
over the pool. The addition of domestic animals must have reflected further participation of the instinctual and feeling parts of
herself. These same animals continued to appear for the next four
sand worlds.

When Ida started to make world 65 (Plate 7) she asked for water

PLATE 7
Sand world 65.

and added it, to make a stream running out of the pool to the right to where the man-woman couple is placed. In the stream she put the same canoe with Indians that she had used in the entry stream in world 46. She said, "I like the security of doing the same thing, and yet feel kind of trapped." So she had experimented with an exit. But at the next session Ida said she hadn't liked what she had done the previous time in making a stream that ran off to the right; it was as if she had become fearful that she might prematurely be letting something from the sacred inner place enter outer reality. She may have felt that she needed to let it work longer in the inner reality. But the fact that she could make the exit at all in world 65 suggests a growing strength to deal with the outer. She returned to the central pool in 66 (Plate 8) and added five sheep and lambs heading down an incline to the pool: the renourishing of the instinctual after the precarious exit. And a knight on horseback, added to the left side in the preceding world, was retained here. The transfer of the knight, who had originally appeared on the right, to the left side may have coincided with her introjecting an animus that had previously been projected. She was no longer so dependent on outer masculine figures.

And now Ida was able to undergo uneventfully the same surgical procedure that had been followed by a psychotic episode five years previously. Her gynecologist had recommended another

PLATE 8
Sand world 66.

D&C in the hope of forestalling the need for more radical surgery. When I went to the hospital to see Ida the evening after the operation, she showed no adverse reactions, and I learned that she was expected to go home the next morning.

Ida returned to my office at her regular appointment time the following week without missing any visits. This one was a talk visit only.

At her next visit, the sand world Ida produced (Plate 9) was similar to the one she had made five days before her surgery (Plate 8), but there is an important addition to the postsurgery sand world: her three children are with her husband and herself. After what she may have experienced as a threat to her child-producing organ, she represents the children she had produced, apparently demonstrating appreciation of her own womanness.

The centered pool had served its purpose in stabilizing her inner being: after the first postsurgery sand world she had no need to continue making pools. And she had no unfavorable effects from the surgery. She had developed a secure inner feminine.

In world 68 (Plate 10) the pool is replaced by a large mound, like the one that appeared in sand world 50, but with no water around it. A treasure is at the top of the mountain and one representation of Ida is standing at the bottom of the mountain. The diving girl is gone and a girl squatting with a trowel is placed with two work-

PLATE 9
Sand world 67.

PLATE 10
Sand world 68.

men to the upper left of the mound. Ida's husband and children are represented, along with another depiction of herself, on the right side (in this picture the children are hidden by the tree). The sitting boy and recumbent girl are at the bottom of the mountain, lower left,

Sand world 69 (Plate 11) is at first glance so similar to 68 as to be barely differentiated from it, but two pieces of turquoise have been uncovered on the left at the bottom of the mountain: one piece by the girl with the trowel, and one piece by the girl and boy. The single woman remains at the near side. Perhaps Ida experienced

PLATE 11
Sand world 69.

newly developing parts of herself as having secured treasures close at hand, making unnecessary the potentially inflationary experience of scaling the mountain.

Ida's 70th sand world was her final one (Plate 12). It consists of almost all the human figures she had used in her previous 69 sand worlds. The torso at top center is the piece she made at home to bring in to an early sandplay session; she had used it often to represent herself prior to this series. The figure opposite it, on the near side of the circle, is a witch. Going clockwise from the torso at the top, the figures are: nun, diving girl, policeman, boy on bicycle, three Japanese women, the Geisha, armed warrior, witch, Robinson Crusoe, Indian chief, Indian squaw with baby, priest, young girl, milkmaid, girl squatting, girl lying on stomach, boy sitting, girl, woman, man, torso. It is as if she had brought all parts of herself, and significant persons in her environment, together in a whole, including various aspects of both the masculine and feminine. In three of the corners, upper and lower right and lower left, are pairs of animals; in the upper left there is a family of five lambs under a tree. So the final form is a squared circle, the form of a mandala, the symbol of wholeness. Ida had come to the end of her sandplay journey.

Ida was to be challenged by one more critical test of her emotional, as well as her physical, stamina. One month after the final sand world she began massive hemorrhaging and had to have an

PLATE 12
Sand world 70.

emergency hysterectomy in the middle of the night. When I saw her the next morning she looked up at me and said, "I'm all right."

Prior to this emergency, in preparation for a five-week absence of my own, I had already arranged for Ida to work with another therapist while I was gone. So after I had paid a second hospital visit two days later, Ida and I did not see each other for five weeks.

Our first visit after my return was largely spent in her telling me how well she had got along. The fact that she could successfully withstand the test of the hysterectomy and almost immediately undergo an extended separation from her analyst had solidly demonstrated to Ida the extent of her new emotional strength.

Ida continued her analytic sessions for several months, consolidating her gains. Some sessions were spent reviewing pictures of her sand worlds, thus bringing the two levels of therapy, verbal and nonverbal, together. I have been in touch with her several times since she terminated analysis with me, and she has not only maintained her gains but has made further advancements. After the breakup of a mutually unsatisfying marriage, she established herself in Colorado and took courses in a field which allowed her to get a well-paid job. She has a close relationship with all three children. She is working on her autobiography—in fact, recently changed jobs in order to have more time available to work on it.

What happened in the 25 sessions after the herself-all-alone-world? I believe they demonstrate sandplay as therapy, not just as pictures of stages or positions of development. The very acts of moving the sand, adding water, repetitiously forming identical backgrounds and adding identical figures; the increasing use of symbols of the feminine; the changing of location of significant figures; the "undoing" of the exiting channel (similar to the earlier unburying scene); all of these experiences contributed to the healing process. The fact that Ida produced so many nearly identical scenes suggests something like a numinous imprinting, brought about by a spiritual involvement.

It is also worth emphasizing again that while this series of sand worlds was being created, our verbal interchange following the sandplay was not about the sandtray Ida had just made and was seldom about her dreams. Our talk was about day-to-day coping with outer things: her husband, the children's activities, visits to her ill parents, misunderstandings with her sisters, the drudgery of keeping house, sexual fantasies and reality, religion, her feelings about me. Often we discussed what she had been reading and sometimes what she had been writing; our relationship supported, and then strengthened, her ego. Another level of analytic work took place in the sandtray. Both were going on contiguously without a direct connection between the two.

The symbolic value of the centered pool was primary in Ida's progress. Its sexual implications may be important: the initial appearance of the pool with its entering channel could be perceived as a symbolic impregnation, and in that case the exiting channel could be symbolic of a birth which Ida experienced as premature. It is quite possible that the pool served as a womb throughout the series. I also see the pool as symbolic of Ida's femininity, not only because of its roundness, but also because it contained water. And water itself is often associated with the unconscious, so the centered pool must have represented both an aspect of the unconscious and an aspect of the centering process.

I think what strikes me most about Ida's sand world scenes is their association with a deep inner core, a sacred place. In compar-

ing the analytic process of unmarried women with careers and
married women like Ida without careers, I have found (Bradway,
1978, p. 41) that the process in both groups typically involves their
withdrawing from an over-extension outside themselves (which
both wife-mothering and following a career can cause) and relating to their inner core, whence these women can eventually go
forth again as the inner achieves validation. I think that Ida's final
25 sand worlds demonstrate this process—or rather are themselves
the process. The protected space provided by the therapist permits
the seeker to find her sacred place.

That the pool was Ida's sacred place is corroborated by her silence about it compared with her volubility about her earlier
worlds, by the placement of treasures in and beside it, and by its
demonstrated healing value.

The fact that the world Ida made after her D&C (Plate 9) was
nearly identical to the one she had made just prior to it (Plate 8) be-
speaks the continuity and security she had discovered in the inner
place regardless of what happened on the outside. It was then that
she could give up making the pool and produce an opposite form:
the mountain. After producing both forms, Ida was prepared to
make her final world in which there is neither a going down into
the earth nor a rising up into the sky, but a staying on the surface
of the earth. The centered circle inside a four cornered form is the
symbol of a squared circle or of the wholeness which she had
achieved. It was after this achievement that she could cope with
emotional threats and take her place in the outer world without
jeopardizing the inner sacred place she had found and in which in-
cubation had occurred.

# A Letter from Ida

*Editor's note: Dr. Bradway sent the manuscript of the preceding paper to
her former patient for comment. Here is part of Ida's reply:*

Dear Dr. Bradway—

I received your manuscript on Friday, and I have read it several times. I want to write right away to let you know how much I like it. Also, I hope you don't mind, but I made a copy of it for myself.

You have written the truth. I agree with everything. Several points which we never talked about were clarified for me. One place was where you refer to the psychotic episode. No one would ever put it into words for me, and I guess I'm glad they didn't. I was better off not knowing. But now I am glad to know it because it explains the irrationality of those times. Also, it is nice to have the whole thing put in a nutshell, so to speak. It seems so simple now.

I am truly pleased and honored to have this study done of my sand worlds. I have learned so much from it—both the general picture as you saw it, and the symbolism of the various characters and creations manifested.

The point of your article is that sandplay *is* therapy. And I agree with you. I feel that it definitely contributes to the healing process. It makes the inner world visible and more readily available for observation, comment, self-knowledge and eventual change. At the time of my 45th sandtray when I was all alone, I was fully aware of the fact that I was getting nowhere. All the scenes were repeating the same thing, and I knew that it wasn't what I was looking for. So I gave up trying. I had worked for so long, and I was tired. And I had no place else to go. I really feel that the opportunity of seeing the same pattern being expressed week after week made me realize that it was futile. I was not aware that my thinking was too rational, but I was aware of the futility of it all. The sandtrays *showed* me that I was presenting theory after theory. And it was done in a comparatively short time. I can't imagine how I could have come to the same conclusion without the aid of the sandplay.

# The Sandplay Process in One Man's Development*

KAREN A. SIGNELL

This paper grew out of my interest in a patient who found sandplay particularly helpful in his individual journey. It is a study of a man who worked through aspects of the mother complex and the father complex in his sand worlds. Its aim is an in-depth understanding of his sandplay process and how it interweaves with his personal history, dreams, and transference, all of which figured strongly in his therapy. Since the paper presents a series of sand worlds which he made during five years of analysis, it also illustrates progression through the major phases of male development, in the way that men's sandtrays often provide such visible landmarks of "where they are" and "where they are going."

BACKGROUND

The patient, whom I will call David, began analysis when he was 27 years old. He was fresh from the midwest and had just begun his medical internship at a hospital. David had a slow, warm smile and was shyly at ease, with the confident bearing often seen in the oldest son of a Jewish family. I could sense his seriousness of purpose, and underneath it a restless spirit of playfulness and individuality—opposites that were to become more ap-

---

*The author wishes to express her appreciation to Drs. Joseph Henderson and Katherine Bradway for their contributions to her understanding of case material presented here.

parent as therapy progressed. David came to therapy firstly because he wanted "more in life than to be a doctor," and secondly to work through his "mother problem."

He was afraid that in the grinding strain of internship and residency he might lose touch with what he called his "more human side"—his compassionate and poetic nature, the dreams that showed him his path in life, and his concern about his place in relation to the mysteries of life and death. He later came to regard these as his creative unconscious core. He hoped also that analysis could help him preserve the things he valued—his capacity to be a doctor, a seeker, and a person with a home life. He was prepared to work at it; despite his hospital schedule he rarely missed a session in the ensuing five years of analysis.

My impression is that David's mother was an extraverted feeling type; she was warm but very critical, intrusive and needy. He bitterly resented her past arbitrary restrictions of his freedom on such matters as dating. During college he had had a brief marriage to "the kind of woman my mother would not pick." It appeared from his history that he had suffered early family suppression of his instincts—sex, aggression, and curiosity, although he had subsequently managed a good adaptation.

David liked and respected his father, a self-made businessman, whom he saw as highly successful in the outer world, and genuinely supportive of his son in his chosen work. However, he did not want to follow his father's pattern of working too hard, and he repressed considerable anger at his father for yielding authority at home to the mother.

At age 9 or 10, he later recalled, there had been a contention between his mother and father. She threatened to leave, and his father gave in. As a result, David said, "I was frozen in fear about any mistakes I might make." My impression is that his father failed him then as a model and that David, too, at that point gave up his aggression and submitted to his mother. At that time, he reported, he had experienced a basic loss of "himself," which he had felt ever since, and which eventually constellated a desire for therapy to restore his autonomy as a person who could lead his own life. It meant that in therapy we needed to deal with early personal history, reclaiming repressed instincts in their fullness as well as his sense of independence. David also needed to reach beyond his personal mother and father to the cultural heritage and the Mother and Father archetypes that gave his parents such strong unconscious power over him, so that he could bring forth, from within himself, the essence of the masculine and feminine principles in new form. It is no coincidence, then, that David was oriented toward the past and toward beginnings—his ancestors, the mystery of life, birth. His greatest fears and awe centered around childbirth and his role as a physician in relationship to such events.

The major theme that sounded time and again in therapy was his existing in the realm of the personal mother and the Great Mother. In counterpoint to this motif was an important second theme—his relationship with his father and the Father archetype, from which he gathered strength. The first stood for connection to the source of the life force—it meant security, and feelings of relatedness to others; the second stood for separateness in the world—self-sufficiency, exposure, movement, direction, setting boundaries and taking risks.

David's main problem, as he experienced it consciously, was his concern about whether what he was doing would please his mother. Her criticism, "You're not good enough," was always ringing in his ears, making him frustrated and angry at himself, since he could never live up to her perfectionistic ideals which he had internalized. I, too, saw this as David's main problem, and I understood it as his having been unconsciously seduced into staying with the Great Mother on an archetypal level, as her son-lover. This was the stage of development to which he returned time and again in therapy. The unconscious was eventually to show him the way out, through the spirit of play and the operation of his own instincts, and the process would be reflected in his sandplay and in the prominence he gave to animals in his sand worlds.

It will be helpful here to remind ourselves of Neumann's (1971) description of the son-lover stage in *The Origins and History of Consciousness:*

> The growth of self-consciousness and the strengthening of masculinity thrusts the image of the Great Mother into the background; the patriarchal society splits it up, and while only the picture of the Good Mother is retained in consciousness, her terrible aspect is relegated to the unconscious. . . .
>
> The situation then is . . . a "good relation" to the mother, but in the gingerbread house of this love there is hidden the witch. . . . Analysis then uncovers the companion picture of the Terrible Mother, an awe-inspiring figure who with threats and intimidations puts a ban on sexuality. (p. 94)

I think that this early stage was reactivated in David's 27th year by his having arrived at an inner readiness to form a new relationship with the feminine—undertaking a relationship with me as his female analyst and, within a month of beginning analysis, falling in love with the woman who would become his wife. This life transition would take him back to his first experience with the feminine—to the trust, mistrust, and engulfment by the mother in the Uroboric stage, and would cause him to reexperience this in a new way with a woman analyst and his woman partner.

We will see how, in David's sand worlds, he revisits the early stages of development and moves on to later ones.* I think of these stages as major themes in a man's life, or tasks he must complete. Rather than visualizing a progression upward step by step, like a ladder, it is more helpful to think of a spiral movement upward as though through a cone seashell, through layers which are all present at the beginning and end. Nevertheless there is in a fundamental way a developmental or stepwise movement. As Piaget (1952) shows, stages in developmental growth are incremental in that

---

*The masculine developmental stages themselves (according to Neumann), and David's progression through them, are summarized at the end of my detailed account of the sand world series, on p. 191. To supplement Neumann's emphasis on the mother complex, however, I have introduced theory on the father complex into my ongoing discussion, when this seemed necessary for an understanding of David's development.

elements in a previous stage are *necessary* for the next; according to Freudian theory, energy brought forward from one stage is *freed up* for the next. From a Jungian viewpoint, there is momentum from behind, but also a teleological or prospective force which is purposive and aims at self-realization or wholeness. Future stages draw one forward.

In Jungian terms all the archetypes and their juxtapositions are present from the beginning and have a basically independent existence, like a cast of characters, but emerge as more or less prominent as a person evolves. One must resolve an archetypal task *enough* at any stage to move on the next. However, a man can also reach forward for help from the anima or self at early stages. In early life, for instance, the anima might be relatively undeveloped as a "mother-anima," "shadow-contaminated anima," or "little girl," but nevertheless helpful. Later, when he is far beyond a stage, he can go back with a more highly developed anima or self and rework the earlier stages. Each broadening of a person's psychological capacity, then, demands the reworking with this new capacity of partially resolved earlier stages. So, too, the same motif can appear in someone's sand worlds again and again, but have a different meaning. One slays the dragon many times anew to free oneself from the mother, to prove oneself to the father, and each time it is a new battle, and each time it is all of the old battles again.

Such a progression of development is easier to see in a series; the sand worlds amplify each other, back and forth. For the sake of exposition, I will make as full an interpretation as I can of each sand world as I present it, both as part of the whole series and in light of my later thinking. Of course, when each sand world was first constructed its meaning was less clear to me and to David, my interpretations fewer, and my understanding less certain!

Over the course of five years, David did 15 sandtrays. I will present 12 of them here. After each sandtray I will quote the explanation David gave of it at the time. The interpretation that follows this explanation includes his later amplification and my own comments in light of the meanings which I see in the images and their general symbolic meaning in Jungian theory.

# Breaking the Container:
# The Uroboros Stage

For the first six months of therapy, David was in crisis. He had
left home and had undertaken many new beginnings: proving
himself at work; finding a mate; and committing himself to therapy.

*The Sea Journey.* His sand world (Plate 1) at the end of six
months looks to me prospective of his launching forth on a journey that will take him into his own life.

> *The man is starting forth with his woman partner* [upper left corner],
> *weaving his way across the ocean, where there is seaweed adrift. He's in a
> sailboat* [upright object just right of center] *led by friendly guides—
> porpoises. He goes past an octopus to the baby* [lower right corner].

The context of this sand world is the ocean, the watery, formless depths of the unconscious where the traveler might encounter
and go past the octopus (archetypal image of the negative Great

PLATE I
The sea journey.

Mother). The water suggests to me that part of David has been slumbering psychologically within the encircling arms of his mother. In this world he is revisiting the images of the maternal Uroboric stage, where one grows through no effort of one's own but feels lost without one's separateness and volition. This stage helps explain David's confidence, ease, and trust in the goodness of life on the one hand, and on the other, his brief anxiety attacks upon leaving home, starting stressful work, and falling in love—in short, his anxiety at having broken the protective container. The deepest ebb and flow between a man and woman stirs up his original feelings of oneness at the watery depths of memory, and of what went well there and what went wrong.

As I understand this sand world, it represents a "quickening" of the unconscious, often seen in early sand worlds when a man begins his therapeutic "journey" to follow his psyche's weaving direction. The unconscious is on the move. Along the way, David will find the "seaweed adrift"—the vegetative or slumbering elements which could be integrated as a passive, receptive, peaceful side of himself to complement his hard-driving side. The sailboat seems a fitting vessel at this point, maintaining his connection to the ocean (the unconscious) but buoying him up on its surface. The power to move is not coming from himself yet, but from the wind, a distant, formless force (the Sky Father). At his side for the journey is a young woman, implying his alignment with a woman partner, a helpful inner feminine figure. She also reflects the therapeutic alliance with me on his analytical voyage as he begins his own version of "the night sea journey" to be born anew from the mother (Jung, 1974).

It is important to notice that he is led by porpoises, suitable animals indeed in their knowledge of the ocean (the unconscious or mother world). They seem to me significantly different from fish: they spring across the water's surface, transcending fishes' confinement to life under the sea, the unknowing world. They are intelligent and also playful animals. They strike me as an instinctual form of the watery puer (see p. 192). They appear to be just what a serious man like David needs to lead him—instinctual wisdom and feelings of well-being, the lighter emotions, the playful and creative spirit. As in sandplay, to play with the unconscious is to allow new life in, to let the unconscious bring renewal. (Of course, a person might eventually need something more aggressive than "friendly porpoises" to accomplish the task, just as one needs more than a disarming smile to free oneself from the clutches of a possessive witch!)

Prognostically, this sand world predicts that David can only reach the baby (a new beginning) if he can get past the entangling octopus—the negative mother. I now see, in retrospect, three aspects of this image: (1) the fearful unknown (the unconscious); (2) the entangling qualities of his real mother, and (3) the potential for feeling entanglement in his relationship with me, and with his new woman partner.

# The Struggle:
# The Great Mother, Son-Lover Stage

During the next year and a half, David's inner struggles reflected a deep desire to be more conscious and free. After "containment in the Great Mother," Neumann calls those in this next stage "The Strugglers." As they become more independent, they become afraid of the mother and are alternately repulsed and seduced by her, and also by their own self-absorption, contentment, and narcissism that keep them inertia-bound.

Neumann (1971) describes the early struggle of a son-lover:

> By differentiating himself from the unconscious and reaffirming his masculine otherness, he very nearly becomes the partner of the maternal unconscious; he is her lover as well as her son. But he is not yet strong enough to cope with her. . . . She is still playing cat-and-mouse with him, and she overshadows even his re-birth. . . . The masculine principle is not yet a paternal tendency balancing the maternal-female principle. (p. 47)

PLATE 2
The panther turns away.

*The Panther Turns Away.* The next sand world (Plate 2) was
made as David finished his internship and began his residency. It is
very helpful in giving us our bearings on the source of his inner
discontent at the time: a revisiting of the son–lover stage.

> *A hungry tiger waiting* [right corner]. *A hurt, whiney self inside the
> fence. I want something from the boy* [center right], *who is offering
> something. The ring: it's hope and a trap. The panther* [lower left] *is
> turning away and leaving the scene.*

"The Panther Turns Away" was David's title for the sand world,
and my general impression from it is that he is denying aggression, his own and others'. The presence of a large feline predator in
a man's sand world suggests to me that aggressive energy is bound
up in the unconscious, and the man himself remote from his full
range of aggressive energy, except for unconscious outbursts.
David sometimes perceived aggression in his mother, woman
partner, or me, but largely denied that also. It was relegated to the
unconscious, and became the terrible attribute of the Great Mother
archetype. Hence, his nighttime anxiety attacks—fear of the pan-

ther and its vicious assaults in the dark. He could not yet confront aggression so that it might eventually be more fully his own. Not being on good terms with either his destructive or creative impulses at this stage, he experienced them via projection.

This failure in being aggressive brings specific consequences, which are illustrated in the sand world: the hungry tiger implies his own natural sexuality and aggressiveness forced into the position of oral neediness and passivity; and the rounded, introverted figure expresses David's innermost core, imprisoned, hurting, and "whiney."

The sandplay often aroused intense affect in David, as it does with other patients, alerting me to the need to explore its significance. Unconscious affect needs amplification and differentiation just as images do, when we are seeking to understand a complex. The remembered tone of repugnance in David's voice when he said "whiney" suggests to me now that he was somewhat conscious of his position and did not like it. Repugnance is a key emotion, a clue that a man may be once again in the stage of the strugglers, disgusted at the mother's greedy seductiveness and withholding, and at his own entrapment. *Whining* may be one result of this struggle, indicating that persistent asking is being met by placation instead of by a real response to the whiner's needs. And of course whining never elicits the desired response either, because the sound contains aggressive tones of which the whiner is unaware. When a son and his mother are caught in this struggle, he needs more than persistence; he needs to state assertively or angrily, "I want," and she needs to give a clear yes or no, so that both can break out of their mutually annoying, unconscious bondage.

There are positive signs in this sand world, however: the young boy figure and the ring. I think what David has constellated here in the sandplay is a strong underlying desire to restore the original sense of himself which he felt he had lost. In a wider sense, the young Krishna offering the golden ball has appeared so many times in early analysis with patients that I think here, too, it refers to the hope that therapy can eventuate in wholeness. Yet with this hope David also experiences a fear that he could merely regress to

PLATE 3
The waterhole.

an earlier state of well-being, confinement within the maternal Uroboros archetype, threatening feelings of ego loss and annihilation. This perception alerted me to transference issues which soon arose between us in therapy: David's potential trust in me and wish to be enclosed and feel love and security; his wish to trust in the flow of the therapeutic process; and also his cautiousness about dependency and his deeper archetypal dread of drowning in the unconscious.

After this, trouble began brewing and David alternated between accepting and rejecting containment within the Great Mother, as we can see in his next sand worlds.

*The Waterhole.* The next sand world, "The Waterhole" (Plate 3), shows jungle animals drinking at a waterhole. A panther (upper left corner) stands nearby, at peace with all the other jungle animals. David said, "The panther could come in and maim the others, but it won't for now." It is a peaceful scene, even if only momentary, showing a nourishing and protective connection with the positive Earth Mother. Apparently David was feeling safe with the woman he was seeing and found therapy a safe container too. I have noticed this "return to the mother" in men's sand worlds, drawings, or dreams prior to risk-taking. It seems to give them the necessary reassurance of basic safety to take a major step. The next week David let go of various women in his life to affirm as his partner the woman he had met and come to love and who eventually became his wife.

For a man, the archetypal break with the mother feels like death. There is a great fear and dread that if he gets too far away, too independent, he will never be able to get back to a secure place again if he needs to. He has to establish this sense of security, as well as tolerance for some insecurity, within himself before he can move on.

*The Pot.* Six weeks later David came into the session overwhelmed by feeling as if he were "in a swamp with tangled trees, alligators, and mists." This time he used sandplay to work through his unconscious feelings as though he were playing out a drama. He first depicted a big tree confined to a small black iron pot which it has outgrown (Plate 4). Then he took the tree from

PLATE 4
The pot.

the pot and planted it in the ground. In subsequent sessions he used this motif to talk about feelings of "being in the pot." The image crystallized for me the realization that he was indeed an "earthbound puer" (see p. 191).

During one therapy session his anger about "the pot" erupted fully when he realized the seductive undertones of his relationship with his mother, and he said "I reject *her!*" with great force. He had become aware not only of his resentment toward his mother's critical side (the bond to the negative mother) but also of his rage about the deeper and more unconscious closeness that is stifling (the bond to the positive mother). David had become independent enough to protest, but not yet to oppose. He saw the problem as largely outside himself—that he needed to accommodate his mother, his woman partner, and me, to avoid any anger.


# Sky Father vs. Earth Mother:
## Manifesting the Masculine Principle


A man with a mother problem needs a counterforce, the masculine principle, to develop his independence. During the next year of therapy the major and minor themes were in interplay. Would David stay mired in the mother world or could he reach into the father world for strength? I am reminded of the preparations in the Celtic myth the *Mabinogion,** before Culhwch could slay the boar (The Terrible Mother). A large proportion of the entire story is given over to vast preparations—the gathering of materials and men for the battle with the Great Mother (Layard, 1975).

For David this was a period of self-doubt, heaviness, paralysis,

---

*The Celtic myth comes rather from my northern European heritage than from David's. However, for that very reason I think it is complementary and explains his sandplay figures. It resonates with the long-lost layers of the primitive, instinctual Earth Mother world.

awe, horror, violence, and hatred. But he also began to find, through his anger, his own energy and movement (the Father archetype) and, near the end, the mysterious moon-path of the anima.

*Too Much, Too Heavy.* This sand world (Plate 5) consists of pairs of masculine figures: two roosters (upper left corner), a lion and the sun (upper left), young Krishna and a monkey (upper left), two sea serpents (upper right corner), and a panther and a leopard at the waterhole (lower right). It is as if David were differentiating masculine qualities into their archetypal or instinctual opposites (for example, lion versus sun). When I first saw this sand world it gave me a hard, empty feeling. Almost all of the animals were of heavy metal (iron, brass, etc.), presenting an appearance of substance and importance, but lacking in life. In retrospect, I wonder whether David was experiencing the hard, empty feeling of men who are swallowed by the devouring Father, that is, who are caught in conventional expectations.

The therapeutic context bears this out to some extent. At the beginning of the session, David said that he had almost quit work in dissatisfaction with the "games" there. He had looked in the mirror and asked, "Am I a good doctor?" He summarized this sand world as a "stale contention" between figures, a contention that was "remote and meaningless." He said, "I'm disgusted with parental 'shoulds'! Life is more important than that!"

There were some small indications of hope and inspiration from the vertical dimension: a feather at the center, and the butterfly (center rear wall) which I saw as symbols of the positive Sky Father and the possibility of transformation.

World 5 is still largely a mystery to me. I think the crux lies in the "two fallen men" (see Plate 6, a close-up of the lower left corner of sand world 5). One man is young; the other old. David referred to them as "father and son." This made me wonder if he and his father were both caught in a heaviness about life, a combination of earthbound puer—the enervation of the youth held down to earth by maternal arms, and Saturn—the old man, orderly and habitual, following the old rules of self-preservation, aware

PLATE 5
Too much, too heavy.

PLATE 6
Close-up of left bottom corner of Plate 5.

of limitations and consequences. The fact that all the animal figures are metal suggests that, indeed, lead invaded the veins of the
earthbound puer and his connection to instinct.

However, the sand world does present a dramatic moment that
suggests new development. David said, "The two figures have
been struck down. Yet they can see the sky and perhaps find some
wisdom there." I myself wonder if they have been overawed by
their first encounter with the Sky Father, the archetypal power of
"something they saw in the sky." That is, whether, with their deep
sense of responsibility, their first response at seeing the heights was
to feel even more earthbound, rather than inspired. It would imply
that later they might acquire more uplifting spirit from the "air-
borne puer" (p. 192) and the lighter side of the Father archetype.

The overall therapeutic significance of this sand world and our
amplification of it was that David sorted out the negative and
heavy aspects of the masculine, so that he could form a relationship to other positive, meaningful aspects of the Father archetype—inspiration, power, movement, wisdom, and spirit. In the
process of such conscious discrimination he was separating from
the mother, the feminine "other," in order to see the world
through his own eyes and differentiate all its other aspects on his
own.

More importantly, he needed to see his personal father as a
model, *differentiated* from his mother's view of the father. In our
culture, in which the father is largely absent from home, a boy's father is often seen filtered through his mother's eyes. She may portray the father's aggression as excessive or inadequate, and may
represent it as merely an extension of her own power ("I'll tell
your father," or "Just wait till your father gets home"). Or she
may portray the father as Saturnine when she is really only project-
ing her own conventionality or her limited masculine ability to
move freely in the world ("Your father wouldn't want you to
. . ." or "You can try it, but I don't think your father would ap-
prove"). I think it is important to sort this out in therapy and help
a man re-connect to his own father.

In making this sand world, I think David was differentiating between his mother's and his father's earthbound and Saturnine aspects, and between the instinctual and the archetypal. This had repercussions in his relation to the collective and the personal.

The sand world opened up his consciousness to a picture of what was happening in his outer life, as his sand worlds often did with their intense affect and images. David was well-liked and respected among his colleagues and, despite some self-doubt about putting himself forward, it came naturally to him to assume leadership in his work. After making this world, however, he extricated himself from a particular leadership position where his anger was ensnared in an impersonal and "stale contention" against the hospital, the collective, while maintaining his values in positive leadership. He made a professional change so that he could work in a place where his specialty would be more respected. He came to terms with what he realized was his unconscious mandate as the oldest son to be "the best or a failure" and made more realistic comparisons between himself and his father.

Sand world 5 also opened up his personal feelings about the argument, when he was 9 or 10, in which his father had given in to his mother. David said that his father had always sided with his mother at home, leaving David alone to challenge her. It appeared that his father had abdicated his role as an independent counterforce to his mother; had, in fact, displayed the typical American father's attitude: "Go ahead and do as your mother says," according to which the home is the woman's territory, and work the man's.

Now David became more open to a new connection with his father; he recalled early experiences when he had seen his father through his own eyes. In consequence he could now see him as strong and also as fallible, and a new personal link seemed to be forged between himself and his father. A man needs a realistic and personal model of masculinity before he can handle the archetypal. David's fifth sand world showed both father and son as needing to look to the sky, to original archetypal power, in order to regain their own masculine energy.

In subsequent therapy, David grappled with an image that had haunted him for a long time—the frightening power of the wind,

Sky Father, whose positive aspect he later differentiated as the Divine Father or spirit. Along with the personal father's authority, this was the very power he needed to move the sailboat (sand world 1).

These inner developments in the masculine realm (relating to his personal father in order to free himself from the more negative aspects of the earthbound puer and Saturnine archetypes; loosening the bonds of always being the "eldest son" to take an appropriate place among peers; opening up to the power of the Father archetype) prepared him to take the next step—an encounter with the Great Mother in her terrible aspect. Like Culhwch, he had enlisted the support of lofty Eiddoel whose help was needed for the boar hunt.

*The Ugly Woman.* A few months later David did a sand world (Plate 7, close-ups Plates 8 and 9) which stands out as highly significant in his development.

*A female head* [object on left] *coming up from the earth. Ugly! I hate it! The lumps on the head are brains. The waves in the sand are from the*

PLATE 7
The ugly woman.

PLATE 8
The Medusa; close-up of Plate 7.

PLATE 9
The Asian figures; close-up of Plate 7.

*head and the whole body emerging. They rock the boat* [center], *which is empty. The "tree in the pot"* [former sandtray] *has become the head, the gargoyles* [upper center] *and the boat. The "two fallen figures" have become the whale* [lower left]. *The "two leopards contending" have become all the jungle animals* [right], *with the elephant as their spokesman. The elephant is trying to reach the bearded figures. The two white bearded figures* [upper left] *are arguing, but it is important, as the seed in the fire-cauldron* [between the two figures] *will grow, and hopefully be strong against the woman.*

The strength of his emotions made it clear that the negative Great Mother had taken form and had burst into consciousness. This sand world is in contrast to the earlier sand worlds that depicted the sea, entrapment, the circle around the waterhole, the root-bound tree—all with their accompanying feelings of vagueness, hunger, contentment, and, overall, confinement in an identity within the maternal Uroboros. Here his main feelings toward the new form (the Medusa) are hatred and loathing, indicating an inner shift of his psyche as the trapped son-lover struggles to gain his independence. As Neumann (1971) observed:

> In the return to the deadly Mother . . . he finds shelter and comfort, for containment in the Great Mother enfolds the child, whether in life or in death.
>
> During the phase when consciousness begins to turn into self-consciousness, that is, to recognize and discriminate itself as a separate individual ego, the maternal uroboros overshadows it like a dark and tragic fate. . . . Now this return becomes more and more difficult and is accomplished with increasing repugnance as the demands of its own independent existence grow more insistent. For the dawning light of consciousness, the maternal uroboros turns to darkness and night. (pp. 44-45)

In succeeding months, as David was thrashing in the thicket to get loose, it helped to have this vivid image from the sand world of what he struggled against—the "ugly woman" or Medusa (Plate 8). This figure also helped me better understand the octopus in the first sand world. The octopus has many arms that hold a person against his will, so that he cannot move away. I would imagine that David's mother did not just cradle him in her arms, but clutched him to her and held him fast, perhaps in first-mother anxiety or so that the baby could meet her needs for warmth and security. The "ugly woman" is a later version of this, the tentacles becoming entangling hair—her mind reaching out like arms to ensnare. During this time David became outraged when, on his visits to his mother, she still came up behind him, put her arms around his shoulders, and called him a baby name, or when she asked questions or said things that felt controlling to him.

In elaboration of the gargoyle figures in the top center of the sand world, he described a dream he had had the preceding week of "a woman patient with a rash all over like cloven hoof marks or imprints. Disgusting. I didn't want to deal with her at all." Although he casually dismissed the gargoyles, his dream suggests their import. In looking back at this sand world now, I think he had separated out the *demonic* aspects from the negative personal mother and Great Mother. These underworld figures are in a central position in the sand world, but they are demarcated by a deep trough suggesting that their power now has limits; and the boat has its point of embarkation from just outside their boundaries, suggesting power wrested from the Great Mother. Now that he is *aware* of her power to ensnare, it cannot sneak up from behind and drag him down to the depths of fear.

As counterpoint to the negative Great Mother theme, there was a strong secondary masculine one. There are jungle animals, with a black elephant as spokesman, trying to reach the two white Asian guardians of the germinating seed. To combat the power of the mother, then, I would infer that his psyche draws on the energy and wisdom of the dark instinctual world as well as on ancestral depths that incubate the emerging hero. This is a development from the earlier sand world, with its metal animals and fallen figures, that he constructed when he was contending with the hospital administration. Instead of responding with brash heroics or defeatism to the old order in its external and sterile forms, he seems here to be cultivating within himself a new order—potentially more meaningful to him, based on respect for the ancient past, natural growth, and instinctual or intuitive knowledge.

The more I look at the two older Asian figures (Plate 9), the more they seem to say. They are foreign or alien to the ego, but at least humanized and relating to each other. They are too white and remote to be reachable by the instinctual power, so they restrain the seeker from connecting with his life force. Nevertheless, they represent the positive side of the archetypal ancestral fathers who preside over the past and also over renewal. In the sand world they are guardians of a well-defined four-sided iron container for the mysterious seed, a differentiated and *masculine* container, as I see it; and its feather or spiritual "temple canopy" suggests further protection for a sacred or royal germinating process.

In looking at the Asian figures now, I am reminded of Culhwch who must first go and submit to his cousin King Arthur and enlist his massive support in order to do battle with the boar and the witch. David, too, could draw strength from his masculine heritage for deliverance as a man from the Medusa's power. He had a strong personal connection to his heritage of the Judaic fathers, so that the archetype of the Ancestral Father and Kingship was naturally constellated in his character. As the eldest son in a strong Jewish tradition, he had connections with his father and grandfathers who maintained and passed on their powers and leadership to him.

In dreams and therapy that followed this sand world, David separated out his father's aggression and authority, ineffectual and positive, and confronted his own potential. As he did so, aggressive outbursts occurred, accompanied by anxiety about "slaying the father." The archetypal base of this anxiety about aggression became clearer several years later: adopting aggression as a man meant giving up his position as a son. Then, no real person would stand between him and the Terrible Mother. Moreover, no personal father would then stand between him and the Divine Father—the awesome realm of spirit, the infinite and death. I think that this is one reason why a man fears to replace his father or a superior: it implies that he will be supplanted next, and will then face his own death and replacement. This phase in David culminated in his accepting from his father a gift that symbolized his own auton-

PLATE 10
Struggle: the sun overpowers the moon.

omy and freedom; and he also became the executor of his father's will; that is, he accepted responsibility beyond sonship.

In most men this sorting out of masculine aspects precedes the appearance of the anima, and it is the anima we shall see in David's next sand world.

*Struggle: The Sun Overpowers the Moon.* A year after the sand world discussed above, David made another (Plate 10):

> *This sand world is called "Struggle: The Sun Overpowers the Moon," although the moon is very powerful. The panther* [left foreground] *is the real danger and he threatens the woman. She's naive, too pure. But the snake* [center, on top of well] *can protect her; he's wise and knows the panther. The well is endless to the bottom. She needs to go down the well, take the snake and dogs* [upper right] *with her, and come out wiser.*

David began this session by referring to the symbolic "Sun" power he had received from his father. I think it was the father's power that enabled him to take this next step, the beginning of his attempts to integrate the feminine side. David was aware that his inner feminine image needed development ("She's naive, too pure"). Looking at this figure now (close-up, Plate 11), I see an un-touchable woman on a pedestal, fragile, inhumanly white. She needs to descend and get dirty, acquire her darker half. In the proc-ess, her unreal idealism or spiritual spell could be broken, allowing more human compassion and a sense of natural balance.

David had dreamed his first "moon" anima dreams. The "true" anima was at first contaminated by (1) images of the possessive Great Mother who, in monstrous form, could harm him; and (2) images of a crazy woman. He became aware that he was talking about relatively unknown sides of himself, and was sorting out ar-chetypal aspects of the Great Mother (devouring and chaotic) and beginning to claim his own anima guide as she took form.

# Fragmentation and Consolidation: Separation of the World Parents

For the next four months, the spring of the last year of David's residency, inner conflicts intensified. In his unconscious he was leaving the Great Mother world he had revisited, a departure which is experienced as a fall or severance from the mother-para-dise and father-god worlds. Neumann (1971) speaks about enter-ing the stage he calls "Separation of the World Parents":

> Naturally enough, as soon as man becomes conscious and acquires an ego, he feels himself a divided being, since he also possesses a formidable other side which resists the process of becoming con-scious . . . until it has finally consolidated itself and is able to stand on its own feet, which, as we shall see, is only possible after the successful fight with the dragon. (p. 122)

David was alternately torn between inertia (staying within the Great Mother) and striking out on his own. Although he overtly placated his own mother, she sensed his growing independence and protested "the look of steel in your eyes." In the father world, he rode the waves of aggression in his dreams and in his occasional

PLATE 11
The woman; close-up of Plate 10.

violent temper outside. He was struggling with the "false fathers," becoming critical of his chief at work and doubtful about himself. He felt torn apart, in anguished indecision about jobs, essentially split between the opposites of seeking too high a position or else working for some doctors he considered "bad doctors." These conscious decisions are battles in the arena of the Father archetype and emotionally, intellectually, and spiritually are powerful experiences for men.

The main way of strengthening the conscious opposition to negative aspects of the unconscious in this stage is through masculine rituals. David spontaneously found rituals and initiation tasks which, for an extravert like him, gave necessary expression and substance to his inner journey. For example, he found an old man to teach him to fish, and he undertook dangerous outdoor feats to experience his strength. He needed "to be among men" and found ways to do this in aggressive sports. He no longer leaped ahead of himself in an extraverted way but struggled with inner decisions first.

At the end of this period he decided what his first job as a doctor would be and made other important decisions in his life. That is, he again passed through the Separation-of-the-World-Parents stage he had experienced as a child long ago, with its feelings of self-doubt, indecision, and defiance, to a state of more masculine consciousness, discrimination, decision-making, and authority. This is a movement beyond passive determinism by others, or by one's own blind or unruly instincts, to a consolidation of the masculine ego.

*Preparing to Go.* He came in one day, announced that he had negotiated a good contract for a job, and made this sand world (Plate 12):

> *A snake* [center] *is going into the well. Doesn't need the bucket. On his own. Into the vast great space beneath. All the figures are oriented toward it. The second snake* [coiled bamboo, upper right] *is leaving the house, a slight imbalance there; and the third is a sea serpent* [right foreground]. *The black dog* [far upper right] *is powerful, safe, and trustworthy, dominating the scene. The little brown and white dog is too cute and warm and tries to run out ahead. The panther* [lower left] *seems*

PLATE 12
Preparing to go.

*more friendly now. He's going to accompany the boat and see that it's okay.
I saw the boat* [center foreground] *first. It has a big prow to withstand
the big waves and the small ones. It'll be okay.*

This sand world is rich in meaning. I am reminded of the *Mabinogion's* King Arthur, finally alone, pressed back by the boar to
his home territory to do battle in his own inner sanctuary. In noting the progression of the panther, we can see that David's aggression now works *for* him. He also has the aid of a *range* of instinctual
aggressive masculine resources—now differentiated into a panther
(wild, instinct-wise aggression), the black dog (semi-domesticated
nature, a powerful ally), and the little dog (overly domesticated nature, too extravertedly friendly, naive, and brash).

A depression followed the making of this sand world; it was
characterized by alternate moments of great anxiety and great
peace, until David finally had a dream that released him more into
his own life. In the dream he asked me (the therapist) a question
and I rejected him. Then, in the actual session, as he struggled
alone to ask me the same question, which he finally did, he broke
out crying. It was as if he were finally facing his fear at age 9 that
he would be abandoned. This uncovered his further fear that he
would *not* be abandoned, but remain possessed by a woman. At
length he fully realized that there was a preferred alternative—to
go and live his own life.

Especially for an extraverted sensation type* like David, this
transference interchange was absolutely necessary. It revealed unconscious emotions and gave them expressive form and validity,
to complement the parallel movement into conscious form of his
underlying inner images in his dreams and sandplay. After this he
consolidated his decisions in two main areas of his life: his first job
(after his residency) as a doctor, and his marriage.

In this fragmentation of his unconscious sense of unity with the
World Parents, David had gone from self-doubt to a sense of his

---

*A person for whom the outer, concrete world and present experience are
important and vivid.

own authority. He wrested from the realm of his personal mother/Great Mother his masculine ego and his full instincts. He aligned himself in relation to his father/Father archetype to take his rightful place among men, and he directed himself to his own destiny.

## The Hero and the Treasure

David finished his final year of residency and reached his 30th birthday.

*Celebration.* The next sand world (Plate 13) heralded a new beginning: a baby on an altar. All the animals were moving in a similar direction, which I see as all the instinctual forces moving in concert toward new life goals. In retrospect, I can also see the baby as his connection to his phallus, his instinctual power as a man, po-

tency, and aggression; and to his new life and direction, creativity, and growth potential.

He saw the animals' destination as "the great unknown," and I think he foresaw a spiritual quest for himself, although his sand world was far ahead of where he was at that time. He spoke again of the self-confidence he had lost when he was young and said that now he had it again, which I understood as an allusion to a sense of regained potency and wholeness, the possession of the Divine Child archetype. With much feeling, he told me about a modern Jewish myth in which the hero accepts the historical era he is in, despite the world's destruction and suffering, because he knows that "the seeds have been sown and will eventually emerge." It seemed to me that David had submitted to the beginning premise of life itself—that life holds suffering and death, and yet can be lived with an underlying faith in meaning or beginnings beyond our conscious knowledge. In this sand world he was reaching forward to the stage of transformation, in which there is a shift from the ego to the self.

*Coming up from the Deep.* Six months later, he did another sand world (close-up, Plate 14):

> *There's conflict. All the animals are railing. Their back ends are stuck in the sand, protesting. The swordsman [center] is afraid to strike the witch [left], to hurt her. But, if he did, his sword would go right through her. She's transparent, ephemeral. There's a father figure [death figure at far left] behind her, and the sharpshooter [figure in center foreground] is aiming his gun at him. . . .*

As I understand the central part of this sand world, David is giving up his unconscious innocence to take action and "slay the dragon," with all his instinctual energies gathered behind him. The array of animals (land, air, water; domestic and jungle) now includes a flying bird signifying his air-borne perspective.

He sees the witch for what she is—an archetype. He neutralizes the power of the death figure behind her (who stands for fear of separation, fear of death). The sharpshooter, whose keen eyesight focuses on a target, represents masculine consciousness and con-

PLATE 14
Coming up from the deep. Close-up of part of a sand world.

centration on what is of central importance. The ability to shoot accurately implies disciplined aggression for attainment of goals.

In the next weeks two dreams carried this partial resolution forward. In one dream David was among various animals all kicking up their feet, at last free from being "stuck fast" in the earth. In another dream, a panther became a big man. The man was holding the hand of a boy, an image which I see as a positive connection between father and son, masculine aggression and puer.

*Balancing* (Plate 15). When David's wife became pregnant, he experienced his deepest inner fears about becoming a father and establishing his own family. The images in this sand world illustrate the mysterious and primitive emotions aroused in a man during his wife's pregnancy.

> The centaur [upper left] *is discarded, almost buried. The horse laments to the moon. The panther* [center foreground] *is near the nest and keeps the dark monkey at bay. The monkey* [right] *could do damage; he's a messenger of the underworld.*

In the background are symbols of sexuality: (1) the discarded centaur, which I see as representing the suppressed animal side, aggressive sexuality and lechery; and its opposite, (2) the white horse who mourns his loss to the moon, representing the pure chivalrous relationship of the knight to his anima.

Sexual issues can naturally erupt on many levels at this time. Pregnancy joins together the sexual act and the sacred mystery of birth, two things that our religions and morality have split apart. Also, a wife may appear self-absorbed, moody, asexual; to understand and preserve sexuality in his marriage, a man needs to sort out how much of this is true of his wife, and how much is his projection onto her. For, at a deeper level, pregnancy brings incestuous feelings into the open. The fact proclaims a man's disloyalty to his mother as son-lover—his sexual union with another and the establishment of his own household. David had a dream of "being caught between two ladies and getting shot, although I was innocent," and he found it very difficult to tell his mother that his wife was pregnant.

PLATE 15
Balancing.

The sand world alerted me as a therapist to problems that can arise during a pregnancy from two important parts of a man's psyche: the sexual lover, who is left half-buried; and the romantic lover, mourning his loss. A man may have to deal with impulses for an affair, or connections with earlier lovers. David immersed himself in work. Then he recognized this as his father's pattern and instead tried to understand the sexual issues in the background of the pregnancy.

In the foreground of the sand world is a panther, representing David's more conscious position. In describing the sand world, David consciously identifies with the panther here in protecting his wife and home by "keeping at bay" the demonic monkey. On a more unconscious level, the panther suggests aggressive, even murderous impulses. A first pregnancy can activate in a man an intense mother transference toward his wife, as well as reactivate all the love and hate feelings he had toward his own siblings.

It is no coincidence that the monkey image appeared at various times during the pregnancy. David, who was very responsive to his wife as well as to his unconscious, was sometimes "drowning" emotionally, identifying with his wife's moods and his image of biological motherhood, especially the inexorable movement of time and "bloody waters gushing forth." He could not fully share her feminine experience, for which she was prepared, psyche and soma, as a woman. He needed a sense of his own masculine "otherness" as a counterforce to succumbing to Earth Mother as archetype. I think the monkey was this compensating *masculine* symbol for him—the free-moving, capricious, profane/divine ruler of chaos and the unknown. The monkey also suggests the transcendent function. As the animal linking man and beast phylogenetically, the monkey is a unifying symbol for spirit and matter.

In becoming a father, David said he felt "like a caterpillar becoming a butterfly." He pondered how to tell his father about the pregnancy, and found that it represented a basic reorientation toward his own father: he would talk to him not so much as a son but as another father and head of a separate household. At the end of the session in which he made this sand world, David spontaneously searched in his mind through his male relatives to find one who was a "good father," that is, a masculine model with whom he could identify in his new role. At the next session, he talked about wanting his "own pace," and he changed the watch he had been wearing for thirteen years. That is, he asserted his own style and mastery in relation to Earth Mother. He was identifying with "ego time" as opposed to the cyclical, primordial time of nature.

## Transformation

*The Road to Change.* During the next year and a half, David's son was born, and he consolidated his therapeutic progression toward a balanced relationship with his own family, his parents, and work. Since then, he has not abdicated his role as father at home, as his own father had appeared to do. Nor has he let his son displace him as the puer, in repetition of the same family cycle. Rather, his son—a robust and energetic boy—has inspired him to leave his earthbound position of hard work to enjoy time at home. He has also worked through shadow material in his dreams, pitting himself against strong, aggressive black men and learning from older, streetwise black men, cunning and subtle.

David was on the threshold of taking a position at work that would be a substantial challenge, when he did another sand world. I will present this final world, "The Road to Change" (Plate 16), briefly to contrast it with his first world five years before, in which the sailboat embarked to encounter the octopus, and his second world, in which the panther turned away, and the ring was "hope and a trap."

> The pack horse [center, between the snakes] *perfectly plodding along, carrying things accumulated for years, those needed. Head down, in a straight line, but not like a train. He could lead off the path if he wanted.*
> *All the animals go purposefully toward the end. It's absolutely right and correct. All want to go, the serpents, dogs, etc. The two dogs [to right*

PLATE 16
The road to change.

and left of pack horse] *protect the horse. I'd placed my ultimate faith in the dogs; they could be vicious if I were attacked.*

*The green serpent* [in front of pack horse] *is old and it's the one I trust. It leads, or else I wouldn't go! In the desert you'd better trust your instincts to get where you're going. The red snake* [behind pack horse] *is new, unpredictable. I need it to protect the rear where I can't see. It's not supposed to bite me; but I'll risk it.*

*The power of the panther has gone into the dogs and the lions* [upper right corner]. *The lions are great! They represent the black panther's changing power somehow. Strong, but pale. It's quiet power in reserve, to be called upon if necessary. The lions are a paler color now, my color, as I'm a Leo. The little figure in the back is new-born, emerging. Same color as the parents. One lies, and one stands apprehensively. It's winter in the forest. Time to give up and prepare for the new. I'm pissed that the lions are fading out, not sure they'll stay out, and I'm afraid to let them go. It's a change time; not a time of death.*

*The old powers are watching. Two statues of strange gods* [upper left, to right and left of ring], *the first you meet. Watch out! Then, two temple buildings close to the gods. Then a strange and unknown negative place inside the ring. Hot or ice cold, dark or weird. I don't want to go there. You can touch the ring.*

*But if you step inside it you're in trouble. No one would. You go around it quickly. Only a blind person would fall into it, the cauldron. It's to get rid of the oblivious, the dead-heads.*

*Then there's a strange and unknown place of royalty, like a king's throne [upper left corner]. It's an old throne, powerful and mysterious. It has a positive charge. A feather [behind throne] marks the end of the road and shades the throne, softening it.*

*The sandtray seems real. They're moving. Cool evening breeze. There's fire in the cauldron and the wind blows. It's smooth; the earth is still.*

The sand world largely speaks for itself. The sense of purpose and correctness in moving toward the mysterious goal, and the concerted effort of the animals, both suggest to me alignment of the ego and instincts on a path to the self; self-realization. The sand world would be too static, complacent, or idealistic in its consolidation but for the potent force for evil—the red snake, who will shake things up when they become too solidified.

# Summary of Developmental Progression in the Sandplay

*Earthbound puer complex.* The concept of the "earthbound puer"* emerged in my work with this patient through the material of transference, dream, and sandplay, and has been helpful in understanding other patients as well. I see the earthbound puer as distinguished in the following ways from the more airy puer usually described in Jungian literature.

A man with a prominent *earthbound puer complex* has a strong unconscious bond to his mother and her approval or criticism, since her love is conditional. He can be close to women and sensitive to others' needs. He is hardworking and responsible beyond

---

*The term was coined by Joseph Henderson in the course of our discussion of this case.

the call of duty. He cares about security and continuity in his life. Commitment is important to him but he approaches it with great caution. Although confident, and usually capable in the outer world, underneath he feels self-critical, trapped, and heavy. It is hard for him to move ahead with his own desires. He is "stuck in the earth," more responsive to others and more reality-bound than he needs to be.

In contrast is a man with a prominent *airborne puer spirit,* whose trust in a positive mother allows him to move more freely and easily as a wanderer or dreamer. He appears lighthearted about realities, idealistic, inspired to transcend everyday difficulties. But he "soars too high" on his mother's hopes for him. He relies on her everpresent cushion when he falls to earth. This leaves him feeling that he is a failure in the world of men, and a failure in his own eyes in finding his own sense of independence and direction in life.

These are complexes in all men, and a man needs some of each. One could also extend these concepts to include a *watery puer,* with unconscious emotional ties to the maternal Uroboros, and the *fire puer* spirit, aggressive, energetic, heroic, and purposive.

David's main complex is the *earthbound puer* and the demanding *negative mother,* who stifles but whose positive aspect is that she spurs him to accomplish things in the world. He is relatively conscious of her effect on his life, and chafes under her criticism, unwittingly criticizing himself for not reaching perfection in relation to cultural ideals. The unconscious part of the bond is that he *wants* to please her and meet her ideals by his achievements. He is "stuck fast" in service to her, rather than to his own life and values.

More unconscious in him is the *watery puer* and his bond to the *positive mother* as her son-lover, a bond characterized by inertia, trust, and occasional angry outbursts. She promises infinite security and demands endless loyalty.

Release from the unconscious mother world first comes through one's instinctual wisdom. It is when the watery puer's rage becomes conscious and takes form, as in the *panther,* that it can liberate him. The panther stands for concentrated aggression, the *fiery puer* spirit. And the earthbound puer is liberated by getting in touch with his independence, his *monkey* or airborne spirit. Throughout this process a man's psyche is drawn forward by forces farther distant—the *Father archetype,* testing and strengthening his masculine consciousness; the *anima,* beckoning him to change; and the *Divine Child-Divine Father* promising wisdom and wholeness.

*Ego Development.* The following summary links David's progression of sand worlds with Neumann's mythological stages of male ego development, and may be taken as a guide to the affects and images typically identified with the respective developmental stages in the sandplay of male patients.

The *Uroboros Stage,* where the *ego is relatively undifferentiated* from the mother and where the individual personality remains undifferentiated, easily slipping back into the sameness of the original unconscious state, can be illustrated by "The Sea Journey" (Plate 1) and "The Waterhole" (Plate 3) with their imagery of watery encirclement. The feeling is both peaceful and vaguely dangerous; the small can be overwhelmed by forces or fate.

In the *Great Mother, Son-Lover Stage,* the emerging *ego struggles to free itself,* as we see in "The Panther Turns Away" (Plate 2) where there is both hope and a trap, and "The Pot" (Plate 4) with its vague yearning to be free. The struggle culminates in the intensity of "The Ugly Woman" (Plate 7) where the Medusa Head appears. Typical sandplay imagery at this stage includes predators, thickets, and entanglement, and is accompanied by feelings of fascination, conflict, repulsion, and paralysis.

The *Separation-of-the-World-Parents* myths recount differentiation of the world into opposites and the *personality becomes identified with the masculine ego.* The "Too Much, Too Heavy" sand world (Plate 5) shows masculine figures in opposition. The feelings that accompany the loss of unity are falling, fragmentation, contention, self-doubt. Then, as the ego consolidates, there are feelings of direction and activity. An example is "Preparing to Go" (Plate 12) where the panther follows the boat.

In the *Hero Stage* the *ego actively moves to separate from the mother and the father* by performing tasks that strengthen the ego, and rituals that build masculine identity. This requires overcoming one's fears, as depicted in the sand world "Coming up from the Deep" (Plate 14) where the swordsman challenges the witch, and the sharpshooter challenges the death figure. Sandplay imagery includes the abyss, mountains, man-to-man opposition or man-to-man alignment; there are feelings of fear and fearlessness, failure and success, restriction and restlessness.

In the *Captive-and-the-Treasure Stage,* a man's ego and libido are freed from the family for his own individual destiny. The *anima* is separated from the mother and *comes into close alliance with the independent ego* as a guide for creative change in the man's life. This higher aspect of the feminine helps him deal with transpersonal forces, an allegiance illustrated in the sand world "The Sun Overpowers the Moon" (Plates 10 and 11) where the anima figure will go into the unknown, not to be dissolved into the unconscious but to bring transformation.

In the *Transformation Stage,* the center of gravity in the psyche shifts *from the ego to the self.* That is, the ego follows the guidance of higher spiritual authority. The sand worlds "The Celebration" (Plate 13) and "Road to Change" (Plate 16) show connection to the Sky Father and wholeness; other sandplay symbols at this stage are those related to spirituality and union, birth and rebirth.

\* \* \*

It is my hope that this case may demonstrate how useful sandplay can be for a patient on his therapeutic journey, and how helpful it can be for therapists in distinguishing the progressive stages of men's development.

This patient came to therapy because he wanted "to be more than a doctor," and because he wanted to work on his "mother problem." He was dedicated to preserving what he valued—becoming a good doctor, remaining a seeker, and having a home life. I think sandplay played an important part in helping him keep in touch with these values and with his unconscious, which brought forth its gifts bountifully in return.

# Are There Any Rules?
## (Musings of a Peripatetic Sandplayer)

GERALDINE H. SPARE

This paper—although of interest, I hope, to therapists already trained in or acquainted with the techniques of sandplay—is particularly addressed to therapists outside the Jungian establishment. Such colleagues have often spoken to me of their intimidation at what they feel to be an exclusivity or even preciosity surrounding the use of the sandtray as a clinical instrument. More positively perhaps—but still with the same consequences for themselves— they express an intense sense of awe and wonder in which sandplay takes on something of the numinosity and power of an archetype of change. Use of the sandtray for these uninitiated, it seems, is surrounded by taboos.

Since in the years that I personally have been using sandplay* both as a patient and as a therapist, I have myself become increasingly interested in the "rules" surrounding its clinical use, I think it may do my non-Jungian colleagues a service to examine these precepts and proscriptions. Indeed they do appear to have grown out

---

*A word about terminology. When we use the word "sandplay" rather than "sandtray" to denote the therapeutic activity, I think there is sometimes a tendency to forget how central the physical presence of the tray itself is in the imaginative experience of making a sand world. It is not out of keeping with the theme of this paper to note here that, frequently, a client's first sight of the sand-filled trays in my consulting room will produce in him or her visible reactions of awe, shyness, or even fright.

of the psychological atmosphere surrounding sandplay; they are largely unwritten; and they seem to present even the clinician with some quite stringent taboos.

Just what are these taboos? Can they be made conscious and rationally examined without robbing the sandplay experience of its numinosity? Can the sandtray itself be demystified, while still insuring that it be treated always with respect and sometimes with awe and wonder?

The "rules" which have evolved can be stated, I think, as follows:

(1) The sandtray is best used in a one to one situation. According to the rules, it is not an instrument that can be utilized in a group. This attitude reflects a basic tenet of Jungian philosophy. Analytic work can best be carried out in the deeply introverted, psychically protected *temenos* of the consulting room. Six or eight other psyches participating in such sensitive work might crumble the walls of the sanctuary.

(2) All the psychic energy and impetus for using the sandtray in the consulting room, it is claimed, must come from the client. The therapist is enjoined from suggesting sandplay. If the therapist suggests that the client work in the sandtray, the patient, sensing power in the therapist, may feel himself in a one-down position, experiencing anger or resistance but wishing desperately to please the authority. He will then be out of touch with his own inner world.

(3) It is best if the therapist never indulges in parallel play in the sand with the client. If this happens, so the argument goes, the therapist's own psychic material may intrude on the client's free expression of his fantasy. Or the therapist's behavior may activate the client's feeling of inferiority or mediocrity—"I could never make a picture as beautiful as yours"—a destructive one-down position for the client.

(4) The client's sand world may not be interpreted or analyzed with him at the time it is made. The construction is to be honored and appreciated by therapist and client together, but it is strongly

suggested that any cognitive stimulus given the client at this time might diminish his emotional experience.

These, then, as I know them, are the prescriptions and proscriptions that have evolved for good clinical practice with the sandtray. I wholeheartedly agree with the thrust of them as guidelines. They are well rooted in the collective experience of Jungian therapists and stem from the Jungian attitude toward psychological change and clinical practice. However, I would like to suggest two other criteria which I find to have a higher value than the precepts listed above. Dr. Clare Thompson* states in her conclusion to the first paper in this volume: "My hope is to encourage therapists of all persuasions to experience sandplay for themselves and to try it for their own purposes in whatever way is consonant with their general therapeutic approach" (p. 20). I find this a very steadying and supportive declaration.

The other criteria to be considered, then, which sometimes contradict or perhaps supersede the rules, are the therapist's psychological type, and his or her emotional centeredness at any given moment of work with the client.

By "centeredness" in the therapeutic situation I mean an intangible assurance more easily experienced than expressed. It rests on two clinical skills: the ability to assess the client's needs accurately at certain critical moments of the dialogue, and to unite with this outer assessment some personal inner clarity about what, if anything, to do. Centeredness implies a willingness by the clinician to initiate action on behalf of the client, the need for which the therapist experiences as arising both from the matrix of the relationship between them and from the energy of their own individual hearts.

As Jungians we are mainly followers. We follow the psychic process wherever it needs to go, knowing that though its route seems willy-nilly or serpentine it is purposeful. But it is my clear conviction that sometimes (though infrequently) we can initiate a process without tearing the fabric of the individual journey. In the

---

*"Variations on a Theme by Lowenfeld: Sandplay in Focus."

paragraphs that follow I share events from my own practice which illustrate my point.

I am a feeling-intuitive type, generally a little more extraverted than introverted. In the pursuance of my clinical practice I have always sat squarely in the middle of the opposites. That is, I see change for myself and for others appearing through the agency of the introverted consulting room *and* the extraverted press of the small group. For almost six years I have invited individuals from my private practice to participate, at roughly monthly intervals, in a group experience which includes five or ten other individuals and a co-therapist. Within this format the sandtray has always been available. It is located in the consulting room, on a floor directly below the group therapy room. The sandtray is introduced as a medium in which participants can play during a specific quiet time of the group experience. The result of this play, the sand world, can be erased and thus remain unknown to other members of the group; or it can be preserved and shared later with me; or the sand world itself in its tray can be brought up to the larger room where the main meetings take place. In the course of almost six years many sand worlds have been shared and many willing hands have helped the sandplayer carry his or her work from the consulting room to the more public place. Not quite so frequently, clients have erased their pictures by replacing the objects on the shelf and instead related the experiences to me in our individual sessions.

At times I have found myself initiating sandplay activity which has produced positive or neutral results. One of my most dramatic failures in this regard was a group sandplay activity which I suggested in preparation for writing this paper. The circumstances of this experience underscore quite clearly the ingredients that are vital to successful therapist-mediated sandplay—and which were absent on this occasion! When I met last with my current group I requested that the eight members make a group sand world. I did not tell them why I needed the sandplay material or that I was interested in their continuing to work in the sand together over six to eight months of the group's life. In short, the impetus for my suggestion did not stem from the matrix of the relationship among us or from any sure knowledge in me that this was what the group needed at this point. Many times before I had suggested group sandplay, and with meaningful results, but on those occasions the suggestion had always originated from a clear awareness in me that it was what the group needed. The results of the present intervention were neutral; that is, the group sandplay lacked the affect and intensity which might enable one or more of its members to move psychologically because of it, or enable the group to have a better understanding of its own emotional components.

Once during these almost six years of group work I broke another "rule" by inviting a new member of the group to play in the sand with me. The new member was a young woman from my private practice. She was at a crossroads where she had to say yea or nay to opposing paths: to training for a professional life in the public arena, or to a seemingly safer, more dependent life in which she could not fulfill her potential. She had a history of loneliness and isolation during the early years of school. At this juncture of her first meeting with the ongoing group she seemed sad, lonely, at odds with herself and restless. As other group members were all individually occupied with their own concerns, painting, writing, and so on in prescribed silence, I was free to invite her to play with me in the sand. She accepted my invitation. She said in a hardly audible voice, "You go first, I don't know how it's done." I went first, feeling very shy and not knowing if it would be helpful to her. My sandpicture focused on four very different aspects of my life which I represented in the four corners of the tray. As she began to work in the second tray she copied my method and became more and more animated and jubilant as she gave order to the elements of her life. I left her alone in the consulting room with her tray and returned to the group. She erased her sandpicture by returning all the objects to the shelves. I have always felt that this experience was a turning point for her. Just recently she reported to me that of all the therapeutic work we had done together this sharing of our two sand worlds was the finest gift I had given her. I have never repeated this intervention with her or anyone else; it has never again seemed appropriate.

And there are other phenomena of my individual practice with the sandtray which I am still trying to assimilate and understand. I initiated sandplay with four clients, one man and three women. The impetus to initiate play came up in me spontaneously and was not part of any experimental design. The clients are apparently all intuitive-thinking or thinking-intuitive types, all but one introverted, and all young adults. All have been in therapy at least two years. All use some variety of obsessive or intellectualizing defense.

Each of these persons seems to me to have been cruelly injured in his or her feeling function almost from the beginning of life; each came from a family where emotion was repressed or so intense that it was not functional. Although the content of the therapeutic hour with these individuals varied greatly, it frequently consisted of an expressive report of the week's events, with varying degrees of externalization and yet a clear sense of suffering.

All four of these clients expressed dissatisfaction with the way therapy was going for them; two asked that I not allow them to "snow" me. And with two of them I made a new contract: in this particular period of their treatment I was to suggest that they work in the sandtray each time they came in. It was agreed that I was allowed to push them in this way, and that they were allowed to refuse my push if it seemed inappropriate to them. With the other two clients, the contract was not so specific; instead, each one made a conscious decision to use the sandtray on every visit for several consecutive weeks, with my very active support and encouragement. Three of the four clients have used the mediation we agreed on to further their journey toward themselves. In the fourth case the results seem equivocal, and I am not yet able to evaluate if the experience for this client was helpful or not. I am going to report here on two of the three clients whose work seems representative of the possible positive effect of this type of intervention.

The first client, Rose, contracted to make a sandtray once a week. Rose had come to me for psychotherapy some five years be-

fore, when she was just returning to work after a short but inca-
pacitating struggle with a severe depressive reaction.

During all our hours of work together Rose had been unable to
remember much of her life before age 11. Up to that time she had
frequently been injured, psychologically and physically, by her life
in an alcoholic household where many strange men came and
went in short relationships with her mother. When she was 11,
Rose had taken her two younger brothers by the hand and led
them away from the house of her mother and the latest of many
"stepfathers" to the house of her natural father and his wife.

Currently, having spent the last year nursing her baby, who was
now about a year old, Rose was trying to decide whether to take a
new professional position, more demanding than the one she had
held before her child was born. She did not know if she should return to work at all; she was very much afraid that her little girl
would be psychologically hurt by her absence from home and the
presence of a strange babysitter.

During her five years of therapy with me, prior to our new contract, Rose had made only one sand world. As she began to work
under our new contract, she reported feeling very tense. She
"couldn't get it right." She chose the wet tray and made rivulets of
water in the sand, requesting more water. She mounded the sand
in the center of the tray, making what turned out to be a "volcano." Right at the end of the hour, almost as she was going out of
the door, she placed on top of the volcano a small figure of Mother
Goose, buried her in the volcano, then brought her to the surface
again (Plate 1).

At the time Rose did not understand the meaning of what she
had done, although she was aware of her contempt for Mother
Goose. Recently, however, she has been able to find words for her
feelings. Mother Goose represented her mother and the false mes-
sage her mother conveyed to her. Rose saw her mother as an intellectual who expressed high ideals of humanism and socialistic concepts, but gave her small daughter little basic nurturance, guidance, or support. She was indeed a "Mother Goose," in that she

PLATE I
Rose's first sandtray. Mother Goose on the Volcano.

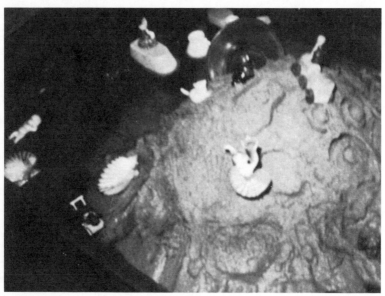

PLATE 2
Rose's second sandtray.

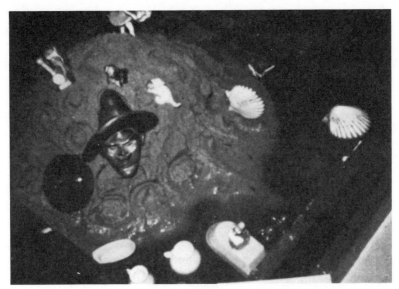

PLATE 3
The same from the frightening side.

told Rose "fairy tales," falsehoods which are now bitter to re-member but were for many years so highly valued (since they represented all her mother had ever given her) that they had come to form an integral part of Rose's own view of the world.

In Rose's next sandtray, one week later, Rose explored her world "before my neurosis" and "after my neurosis" (Plates 2 and 3). The side of the tray which represents "after" (right-hand side of Plate 2) is almost empty, because that aspect of her life was still building. The "before" side, the frightening side (top and left of Plate 2, bottom and right of Plate 3), depicts Mother Goose sitting on an overturned bathtub spinning her false stories. Also on the frightening side is a darkfaced man in a big hat, representing Rose's stepfather and her mother's many male visitors, some of whom hurt the little girl. There are also some little playthings, a child's small broom and toy baby carriage, representing the few, precious gifts Rose recalls ever receiving as a child—gifts from grandparents she never saw after she was two.

Most important of all, in this sandtray Rose discovered a black baby and a white baby (against the right hand edge of the tray,

Plate 3), opposing parts of herself which in their conflict worked against her: the black child, the "protector," was a fighter, at times excessively aggressive and defensive, who was jealous of the white child's ability to feel. The white child was gentler, in touch with her feelings and timid; she could not value the black child's assertiveness.

Rose's next sand world (Plate 4), made one week later, depicts the resolution of her conflict about returning to professional work. The picture is very orderly: home is on the right, work on the left. Her new little baby is safe in its crib (right side center), and the white and black babies are lying together (bottom left corner of the "home" division) watching TV—an indication of a beginning integration. The dragon represents the bridge Rose drives over twice a day from home to work and back. The bridge represents better connections, not only between Rose's personal and professional life, but between her past and her present; between her own

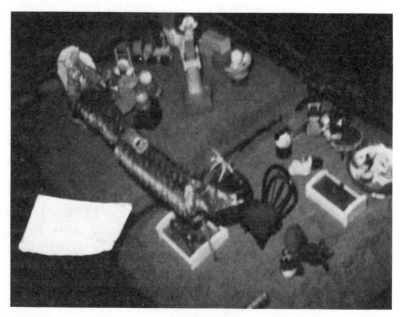

PLATE 4
Rose's third tray. Home and work.

PLATE 5
Helen's first world after the "earthquake."

mother, herself as infant and child, herself as mother, and her own
new baby. The sand world speaks eloquently of the healing that
has taken place in Rose's psyche.

My contract with the second client, Helen, called for me to suggest that she work in the sandtray during every therapy hour. Hel-
en's first sand world under the new rules was a very carefully integrated and complex representation of her life. After she had made
it she said, "This is part of why I always feel like crying. Seems as
if there's a part of me that I can't read, that has to do with the black
and the white." In response to this observation I said, "Looks like
maybe you're feeling pretty angry. I wonder if there's anything
you'd like to do with the anger." Plates 5, 6 and 7 depict what she
did with the anger. The nude form of a woman is toppled, the
miniature clock is askew, a dump truck is set on its side. The only
things really remaining upright and solid are a sturdy house and
two boats, a steamer and a little sailboat. Not one sandplay item
was injured in this earthquake, but the client's whole world was
turned topsy-turvy. The sand world she made immediately after-

PLATE 6
The same, another view.

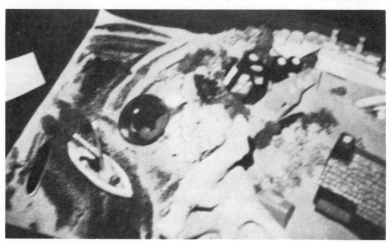

PLATE 7
The same, a third view.

ward in the same session is shown in Plate 8. She was offered and accepted the use of water in making this second picture, and she used a great quantity of it. There are islands and inlets and converging streams. Five trees are placed peacefully on the islands in the water. Permission to destroy her first world with an earth-

PLATE 8
Helen's second world, same session.

quake seemed to settle Helen's inexorably intrusive, obsessional thoughts and allow her a quiet moment. Where all was immeasurably complex, all is now simplicity and there is a wholesome lack of clutter. Helen smiled and seemed relaxed. We agreed that she had experienced the constructive building impetus within her and that destructive, angry forces had shaken her world to its very source. She had felt some new beginning in the flood of waters and the five peaceful trees.

Since this event I have only once suggested that Helen make a sandtray. It is my feeling that she is now making good progress in facing the inner monsters which shook up her world. Her therapy is again in her own hands.

This concludes my experiences of breaking the taboos of sandplay—experiences which so far have assured me that there are no absolute rules on how to use the medium of sandplay in psychotherapy. Timing seems to be crucial. Intervention of the kind I describe may be needed only once in the course of the long spiral of psychic change. But such an intervention may represent a focal point in the therapeutic relationship, at which, for a short time, the innovative energy of the therapist is lent to the client, in much the same way that at times we lend our egos and share such life experiences as may be helpful.

As with every aspect of clinical practice, meaningful use of sandplay is a function of our own human hearts, and of the ever ongoing interplay between our own centers and the centers, hearts, and needs of those we are privileged to see in psychotherapy.

# References

Aite, Paolo. Ego and image: Some observations on the theme of "sandplay." *Journal of Analytical Psychology*, 1978, *23*, 332-338.

Albino, Ronald C. Defenses against aggression in the play of young children. *British Journal of Medical Psychology*, 1954, *27*, 61-71.

Ames, Louise Bates and Learned, Janet. Imaginary companions and related phenomena. *Journal of Genetic Psychology*, 1946, *69*, 147-167.

Aries, Phillippe. *Centuries of childhood: A social history of family life.* New York: Knopf, 1962.

Blurton-Jones, N. G. An ethological study of some aspects of social behaviour of children in nursery school. In Desmond Morris (Ed.), *Primate ethology.* Garden City, New York: Anchor Books, 1969.

Blurton-Jones, N. G. Categories of child-child interaction, In N. G. Blurton-Jones (Ed.), *Ethological studies of child behaviour.* Cambridge, England: Cambridge University Press, 1974.

Bolgar, Hedda and Fischer, Liselotte. Personality projection in the World Test. *American Journal of Orthopsychiatry*, 1947, *17*, 117-128.

Bowyer, Laura Ruth. The importance of sand in the World Technique: An experiment. *British Journal of Educational Psychology*, 1959, *29*, 162-164.

Bowyer, Laura Ruth. *The Lowenfeld World Technique.* Oxford: Pergamon Press, 1970.

Bradway, Katherine. Hestia and Athena in the analysis of women. *Inward Light,* XLI, 91, Spring 1978, 28–42.

Caillois, Roger. *Man, play and games.* New York: The Free Press of Glencoe, 1961.

Cramer, Phebe and Hogan, Katherine. Sex differences in verbal and play fantasy. *Developmental Psychology,* 1975, *11,* 145–154.

Dahlgren, Barbro. *The World Test. Research Bulletin No. 11.* Stockholm: University Institute of Education, 1957.

DeMause, Lloyd (Ed.). *The history of childhood.* New York: Harper and Row, 1975.

Eickhoff, Louise F. W. Dreams in sand. *British Journal of Psychiatry,* 1952, *98,* 235–243.

Erikson, Erik H. Sex differences in the play configurations of pre-adolescents. *American Journal of Orthopsychiatry,* 1951, *21,* 667–692.

Erikson, Erik H. *Childhood and society* (2nd Rev. ed.). New York: W. W. Norton, 1963.

Erikson, Erik H. Inner and outer space: Reflections on womanhood. *Daedalus,* 1964, *93,* 588–597.

Flavell, John H. *The developmental psychology of Jean Piaget.* New York: D. Van Nostrand, 1963.

Gould, Rosalind. *Child studies through fantasy.* New York: Quadrangle Books, 1972.

Goulet, Jacques. The infant's conception of causality and his reaction to strangers. In Therese Govin Decarie (Ed.), *The infant's reaction to strangers.* New York: International Universities Press, 1974.

Guntrip, Henry J. *Schizoid phenomena, object-relations, and the self.* New York: International Universities Press, 1968.

Halliday, Michael Alexander K. *Learning how to mean: Explorations in the development of language.* London: Edward Arnold, 1975.

Henderson, Joseph Lewis. Analytical psychology in England. *Psychological Perspectives,* 1975, *6,* 197–203.

Homburger, Erik. Dramatic productions test. In H. A. Murray (Ed.), *Explorations in personality.* New York: Oxford University Press, 1938, 553–4.

Huizings, John. Homo ludens: The play element in culture. London: Routledge and Kegan Paul, 1949.

Hutt, C. Exploration and play in children. Symposium of the zoological society of London, 1966, 18, 61-81.

Jones, Richard Matthew. Ego synthesis in dreams. Cambridge, Mass.: Schenkman Publishing, 1962.

Jones, Richard Matthew. Fantasy and feeling in education. New York: Harper Colophon Books, 1968.

Jung, Carl Gustav. Memories, dreams, reflections. New York: Pantheon Books, 1961. Also New York: Vintage Books, 1965.

Jung, Carl Gustav. Collected works. Princeton: Princeton University Press, Vol. 5 (2nd ed.), 1967; Vol. 6, 1971; Vol. 7 (2nd ed.), 1966; Vol. 8 (2nd ed.,), 1972; Vol. 9 (2nd ed.), I, 1968(a), 11, 1968(b); Vol. 16 (2nd ed.) 1975.

Kalff, Dora M. The archetype as a healing factor. Psychologia, 1966, 9,177184.

Archetypus als heilender Faktor. In A. Guggenbuhl-Craig (Ed.), Der Archetyp. Verb. 2. Int. Kongr. Analyt. Psychol., Zurich, 1962,182-200. New York: S. Karger, 1964.

Kalff, Dora M. Sandplay: Mirror of a child's psyche. San Francisco: Browser Press, 1971. (Republished as Sandplay: A psychotherapeutic approach to the psyche. Boston: Sigo Press, 1981). Sandspiel. Zurich: Rascher, 1966.

Klinger, Eric. Structure and function of fantasy. New York: John Wiley & Sons, 1971.

Laing, Ronald D. The family and the "family." The politics of the family and other essays. New York: Vintage Books, 1972.

Layard, John. A celtic quest: Sexuality and soul in individuation. Zurich: Spring Publications, 1975.

Lowenfeld, Margaret. The World pictures of children. A method of recording and studying them. British Journal of Medical Psychology, 1939,18, 65-101.

Lowenfeld, Margaret. The nature and use of the Lowenfeld World Technique in work with children and adults. Journal of Psychology, 1950, 30, 325-331.

Lowenfeld, Margaret. The World Technique. Topical Problems in Psychotherapy, 1960, 3, 248-263.

Lowenfeld, Margaret. *Play in childhood*. New York: John Wiley & Sons, 1967. (Originally published 1935.)

Lowenfeld, Margaret. *The World Technique*. London: George Allen & Unwin, 1979.

Matthiessen, Peter. *Under the mountain wall*. New York: Ballantine Books, 1969.

Mattoon, Mary Ann. *Applied dream analysis*. New York: V. H. Winston & Sons, 1978.

Neumann, Erich. *The origins and history of consciousness*. Vols. I and II. New York: Harper Torchbooks, 1962. Princeton, New Jersey: Princeton University Press, 1971.

Neumann, Erich. *The child*. New York: G. P. Putnam's Sons, 1973.

Noel, Daniel C. Veiled kabir: C. G. Jung's phallic self-image. *Spring 1974, 238,* 229-230.

Piaget, Jean. *The origins of intelligence in children*. New York: International Universities Press, 1952.

Piaget, Jean. *Play, dreams and imitation in childhood*. New York: W. W. Norton, 1962.

Piaget, Jean *Six psychological studies*. New York: Vintage Books, 1968.

Piaget, Jean. *Genetic epistemology*. New York: W. W. Norton, 1970(a).

Piaget, Jean. *Main trends in psychology*. New York: Harper Torch books, 1970(b).

Piaget, Jean and Inhelder, Bärbel. *The psychology of the child*. New York: Basic Books, 1969.

Pickford, Ruth. The versatility of the World Technique. *Projective Psychology, 1973, 18,* 21-23.

Reese, Hayne W. and Overton, W. F. Models of development and theories of development. In L. R. Goulet and P. B. Baltes (Eds.), *Life-span developmental psychology*. New York: Academic Press, 1970.

Roberts, John M. and Sutton-Smith, Brian. Child training and game involvement. *Ethnology,* 1962, *1,* 166-185.

Rosenberg B. G. and Sutton-Smith, Brian. The measurement of masculinity and femininity in children: An extension and revalidation. *Journal of Genetic Psychology,* 1964, *104,* 259-264.

Schwartzman, Helen B. *Transformations: The anthropology of children's play.* New York: Plenum Press, 1978.

Spencer, Mary Jo. The loss of the sacred object. *Professional reports. Sixth Annual Conference of the Societies of Jungian Analysts of Northern and Southern California.* San Francisco: C. G. Jung Institute, 1979, 55-58.

Stein, M. The devouring father. *Fathers and mothers.* New York: Spring Publications, 1973.

Stewart, Louis H. Sandplay therapy: Jungian technique. In B. B. Wolman (Ed.), *International encyclopedia of psychiatry, psychology, psychoanalysis and neurology.* Vol. 10, 9-11. New York: Aesculapius Publishers, 1977.

Sutton-Smith, Brian. Play, games and controls. In John Paul Scott and Sarah F. Scott (Eds.), *Social control and social change.* Chicago: Chicago University Press, 1971(a).

Sutton-Smith, Brian. The playful modes of knowing. In *Play: The child strives toward self-realization.* Washington, D.C.: National Association for the Education of Young Children, 1971(b).

Sutton-Smith, Brian. A syntax for play and games. In Robert Ernest Herron and Brian Sutton-Smith (Eds.), *Child's play.* New York: John Wiley & Sons, 1971(c).

Sutton-Smith, Brian. *The folk-games of children.* Austin, Texas: University of Texas Press [1972].

Sutton-Smith, Brian and Sutton-Smith, Shirley. *How to play with your children (and when not to).* New York: Hawthorne Books, 1974.

Sutton-Smith, Brian. Excerpts from The dialectics of play. *The Association for the Anthropological Study of Play Newsletter,* 1976, *3.*

Sutton-Smith, Brian. A sociolinguistic approach to ludic action. In H. Lenk (Ed.), *Handlungentheorien Interdiszipliner,* Vol. 3. Karlsruhe, West Germany: Universität Karlsruhe, 1977(a).

Sutton-Smith, Brian. Towards an anthropology of play. In P. Stevens (Ed.), *Proceedings of the Second Annual Meeting of the Association for the Anthropological Study of Play.* West Point, New York: Leisure Press, 1977(b).

Sutton-Smith, Brian. Games of order and disorder. *The Associa-tion for the Anthropological Study of Play Newsletter,* Vol. 4, 2, 22, Fall 1977(c).

Tanner, John M. and Inhelder, Bärbel. *Discussions on child develop-ment.* Vol. 4. New York: International Universities Press, 1960.

Thompson, Ernestine H. and Johnson, Tanya F. The imaginary playmate and other imaginary figures of childhood. In P. Ste-vens (Ed.), *Proceedings of the Second Annual Meeting of the Associa-tion for the Anthropological Study of Play.* West Point, New York: Leisure Press, 1977.

Vitale, A. Saturn: The transformation of the father. *Fathers and mothers.* New York: Spring Publications, 1973.

Wells, Herbert George. *Floor games.* New York: Arno Press, 1975. (Originally published, 1911 in England. First American edition, Boston, 1912.)

Winnicott, Donald Woods. *The maturational process and the facilitat-ing environment.* London: Hogarth Press, 1965.

# Reference Notes

1. Garner, Ann Margaret. Personal communication with Clare Thompson, 1978.
2. Mucchielli, Roger. *Le jeu du monde et le Test du Village Imaginaire*. Paris: Presses Universitaires de France, 1960. Relevant chapters available through the library of the C. G. Jung Institute of San Francisco.
3. Paterson, Elspeth A. *An investigation of some European nations using "The Village Technique."* Unpublished master's thesis, University of Glasgow, 1968. Relevant chapters available through the library of the C. G. Jung Institute of San Francisco.
4. Kamp, J. M. J. and Kessler, E. S. *The World Test: Preliminaries to a developmental scale.* Utrecht. Unpublished manuscript, 1967.
5. Bernhardt, Ann. Personal communication with Clare Thompson, 1976.
6. Stewart, Louis H. and Stewart, Charles T. *Play, games and affects: A contribution toward a comprehensive theory of play.* Paper presented at the Annual Meeting of the Association for the Anthropological Study of Play, 1979.
7. Stewart, Charles T. and Stewart, Louis H. *Play, games and stages of development: A contribution toward a comprehensive theory of play.* Unpublished manuscript, 1979.
8. Thompson, Clare. Personal communication with Karen Signell, 1979.

# Selected Annotated Bibliography

CLARE THOMPSON AND PAUL WILTSE

We wish to acknowledge a grant from the Ernst and Eleanor van Löben Sels Scholarship Fund of the C. G. Jung Institute of San Francisco, which made possible two separate computer searches of the literature. We wish also to acknowledge the expert help of the people conducting those searches: Sonya Kaufman, Education-Psychology Library, University of California, Berkeley; and Siegfried Clemens, Technical Information Specialist, National Clearinghouse for Mental Health Information, N.I.M.H.

It is suggested that anyone working in this field become familiar with these twenty-nine references. They have been selected not only for excellence but also for accessibility. Thus foreign language publications are included only where there has also been publication in English. With one exception, all publications we found by members of the International Association for Analytical Psychology (I.A.A.P.) are included. That exception is H. Kawai's *An Introduction to the Sandplay Technique* which is written in Japanese. The Fujii reference in a British journal is the one we found most helpful with the Japanese literature. The I.A.A.P. members whose publications are listed below are Aite, Bradway, Kalff and L. H. Stewart.

Aite, Paolo. Communication through imagination. *Annual of Italian Analytical Psychologists*, 1977, *1*, 105-130.
*Rivista di Psicologia Analitica*, 1976, *7*, 102-129.
A detailed consideration of a tray made by an adult patient as an example of how Aite works on such material. Aite sees the meth-

od as facilitating communication and, probably to a greater extent than most sandplay therapists, emphasizes the spatial aspects of the construction. Included is his subjective experience while with a patient who is making a picture.

Aite, Paolo. Ego and image: Some observations on the theme of "sandplay." *Journal of Analytical Psychology,* 1978, *23,* 332-338.
Differentiates between Jung's technical term "active imagination" and imaginative activity, which is what Aite thinks operates in sandplay. Describes with considerable detail how he goes about the (nonvoiced) interpretation of a particular tray. The color photograph and the sketch of this tray illustrate very well the advantages of each method of recording.

Bolgar, Hedda and Fischer, Liselotte. Personality projection in the World Test. *American Journal of Orthopsychiatry,* 1947, *17,* 117-128.
A group of one hundred adults, educationally and socio-economically somewhat above average, made individual sandtray worlds. The reported results may provide good normative data. The article refers to crosscultural studies showing only negligible differences between Central Europe, Brazil, and the United States. These data would be important, for if such groups do not differ from each other, then perhaps the data in this article may still provide usable norms thirty years later, but efforts by the present bibliographers to obtain the data from these crosscultural studies have been unsuccessful. A workable scoring system is presented.

Bowyer, Laura Ruth. The importance of sand in the World Technique: An Experiment. *British Journal of Educational Psychology,* 1959, *29,* 162-164.
Finds from a review of over 300 sandtray worlds made by people not in psychotherapy, that "sand can be used constructively, expressively, symbolically, or destructively; can be ignored except as a base; or can be reacted against, to the extent of covering it over with cardboard." The use of sand is traced developmentally, and is seen as similar to M in the Rorschach. Special attention is given to the activity of burying objects in the sand.

Bowyer, Laura Ruth. *The Lowenfeld World Technique.* Oxford: Pergamon Press, 1970.
An invaluable reference work. Gives the origins of the method and describes its use. Also abstracts at some length the wide, largely European, literature to date. Introduction by Margaret Lowenfeld.

Bradway, Katherine. Initial and final sandplay worlds of married non-career and unmarried career women in analysis. *Professional Reports. Sixth Annual Conference of the Societies of Jungian Analysts of Northern and Southern California* (short title). San Francisco: C. G. Jung Institute, 1979, 35–41.
Presents the sandplay worlds of five home and five career women making initial sand worlds with the writer between 1969 and 1973. Traces the background and use of the method, as well as the writer's understanding of women in terms of the goddesses Hestia (Vesta) and Athena. Although no type differences between the two groups were found at first, their initial sand worlds did differ in ways consistent with their group membership. The final sand worlds of the two groups show more overlapping than do the initial sand worlds. The writer concludes with the relation, as she sees it, of analytic practice to research.

Bradway, Katherine. Sandplay in psychotherapy. *Art Psychotherapy,* 1979, *6,* 85–93.
Starts with an excellent description of the method, how it developed, how it is used and what makes it effective. Two contrasting cases are then presented to demonstrate these points. The rest of the paper deals with the questions "To what extent do the sand scenes reflect progress in therapy?" and "To what extent do they effect the progress, i.e., to what extent are they therapy?"

Bühler, Charlotte. The World Test. Manual of directions. *Journal of Child Psychiatry,* 1951, *2,* 69–81.
Replaces the Manual published by the Psychological Corporation in 1940. The best single reference to this "projective technique making use of the fact that people like to build things and that their constructions express their personalities." (A whole literature on

this diagnostic method exists, not covered in this bibliography, but see the Appendix).

Cramer, Phebe, and Hogan, Katherine A. Sex differences in verbal and play fantasy. *Development Psychology,* 1975, *11,* 145-154
Replicates Erikson's work with preadolescents and results in the same findings thirty-five years later. Also studied were boys and girls entering school, and the findings held true for these younger children. When verbal fantasy material was used, results for the preadolescent girls and boys differed, but for the younger children they did not. The persistence of Erikson's findings is especially impressive in view of changes in how women viewed themselves in 1940 and 1975.

Dundas, Evalyn. *Symbols come alive in the sand.* Originally privately printed, but now available in a revised and expanded version. Boston: Sigo Press, 1980.
An engaging book in which a therapist with Jungian orientation outlines how she uses and sees sandplay. Five boys and three girls from her practice are presented; the expanded version also includes the case study of a woman patient. The final chapter illustrates how the Jungian orientation works. The writer has so frequently encountered the bear and the owl in the sandplay of children that she did library research on both symbols. Her findings are presented, presumably because other therapists may be having the same experiences. Excellent sketches.

Eickhoff, Louise F.W. Dreams in the sand. *British Journal of Psychiatry,* 1952, *98,* 235-243.
The only paper on sandplay by this writer, this is a real treasure trove. She finds the sandtray world "the most therapeutically exciting and satisfying medium in my experience" and writes about it with excitement. One gains a good picture of what she does (a more active participation than characteristic of most sandplay therapists), and how she understands the spatial aspects of the constructions, especially when they are viewed serially. It is the best illustration we know of that the method is not tied to any one orienta-

tion. She found, for example, condensation and secondary elaboration, and concludes: "Freud points out that the essence of the dream function is regressive, as it implies a translation of the wish into an archaic form of language, and surely the most archaic of all expression is the concrete representation, as we can have in the sand tray."

Erikson, Erik H. Sex differences in the play configurations of preadolescents. *American Journal of Orthopsychiatry,* 1951, *21,* 667-692.
An account of the play constructions of preadolescent girls and boys done as part of the Berkeley Guidance Study in 1939 through 1941. Although his task was to make observations of individual boys and girls, to be collated with those from other methods, he was soon struck by ways which characterized girls but not boys, and boys but not girls. This, like Lowenfeld's work, is an illustration of what can come from empirical observation. Some of these findings were also published in *Childhood and Society* (New York: Norton, 1963).

Erikson, Erik H. Inner and outer space: Reflections on womanhood. *Daedalus,* 1964, *93,* 558-597. (Also published as Womanhood and the inner space, in J. Strouse (Ed.), *Women and analysis.* New York: Grossman Publishers, 1974, 297-306; and in Erikson, Erik H., *Identity: Youth and crisis.* New York: W. W. Norton, 1968, 268-279.)
In this article on the psychology of women, the findings on play constructions of preadolescent girls are recounted, as is their development into his new formulation on women's psychology.

Fujii, Shinobu. Retest reliability of the sandplay technique (1st report). *The British Journal of Projective Psychology and Personality Study,* 1979, *24,* 21-25.
This article puts the work of Japanese therapists in context. "From ancient times Japan has had a traditional formative art called 'Hakoniwa'. Hakoniwa consists of small, mostly oval, trays and mini-

atures of scenery. Man arranges trees, houses, stones, white sand, etc. and lays out a landscape in it, which indicates a mental world of harmony in common with the spirit of Zen." Five research studies published in Japanese are then reviewed and mention is made of numerous clinical case studies. The body of the article is concerned with the ability of judges to match sandtray worlds made two weeks apart. Trained judges performed significantly better than chance and significantly better than students. "But why experienced people can use the S[and] P[lay] T[echnique] much more accurately is another question which needs further study."

Homburger, Erik. Dramatic productions test. In H. A. Murray (Ed.), Explorations in personality. New York: Oxford University Press, 1938, 553-4.
This break-through in psychological methodology includes a section by Erikson on dramatic productions. Although sand is not a part of the method, in common with sandplay it uses a confined space, miniatures, and blocks. A 1937 article ("Configurations in Play-Clinical Notes," Psychoanalytic Quarterly, 6, 139-214) reports these results also.

Kalff, Dora M. The archetype as a healing factor. Psychologia, 1966, 9, 177184. Archetypus als heilender Faktor. In A. Guggenbuhl-Craig (Ed.), Der Archetyp. Verb. 2. Int. Kongr. Analyt. Psychol., Zurich, 1962,182-200. New York: S. Karger, 1964.
Presented in 1962 to the Second International Congress of Analytical Psychology in Zurich, this paper outlines Neumann's development of the self and illustrates it with two cases, which are also in Sandplay (below). The value of the method is seen as allowing the child to play out his imagination within a bounded and confined space. The analyst understands the inner situation through its symbolic representation, and this play of imagination influences the dynamics of the unconscious in the child.

Kalff, Dora M. Sandplay: A psychotherapeutic approach to the psyche. Boston: Sigo Press, 1981.

Sandspiel. Zurich: Rascher, 1966.
The first chapter is the writer's clearest published statement of her position. To read at least this one chapter is a must for anyone interested in the method. It is followed by a series of cases, including that of one adult. The introduction by Harold Stone should be read first, as a setting.

Lowenfeld, Margaret. Play in childhood. London: Victor Gollancz, 1935. New York: John Wiley & Sons, 1967.
An historically important book not published in this country until 1967. All aspects of play are covered; the chapter "Play as a demonstration of phantasy" is the most germane to the present volume. Only one publication by Lowenfeld–as child-psychotherapist predates this ("A New Approach to the Problem of Psychoneurosis in Childhood." British Journal of Medical Psychology, 1931, 11, 194-227).

Lowenfeld, Margaret. The world pictures of children: A method of recording and studying them. British Journal of Medical Psychology, 1939, 18, 65-101.
An important paper, presenting for the first time what came to be known as the World Technique, as delivered to the Psychology Section of the British Medical Society. Although the 1979 book covers the same ground, there is much to be gained by reading her work chronologically.

Lowenfeld, Margaret. The nature and use of the Lowenfeld World Technique in work with children and adults. Journal of Psychology, 1950, 30, 325-331.
This address to an American audience starts with a description of ICP and the work done there. Lowenfeld expounds her findings on children's thinking, and outlines the World Technique as a method of expressing this thinking. The derivation of a test from this method is explored.

Lowenfeld, Margaret. The World Technique. *Topical Problems in Psychotherapy,* 1960, *3,* 248-263.
The writer's summary begins, "The essential focus of psychother-apy is communication; communication of one aspect of the patient to another within himself and from the patient to the therapist. A brief description is given of a technique of intra- and interpersonal communication called the World Technique" (p. 262). Illustrative case material is presented. The reader is struck by how "Jungian" it sounds: not only are symbols stressed, but one reads "We no-ticed certain recurring features suggesting more than a personal or individual content."

Lowenfeld, Margaret. *The World Technique.* London: George Allen & Unwin, 1979.
A must for anyone using the method, this posthumous book brings together Lowenfeld's work through 1960. Her introduction is recommended, especially pages 16-20 where she describes what she is later to call the "protosystem"—children's thinking as she sees it. Her idea of "outside of time and space" again seems very "Jungian." Three cases give a good picture of how she worked. Unique in our reading is the final chapter "On the subjective mak-ing of a World," where adults describe their experience with sand-play and where it led.

Mucchielli, Roger. *Le jeu du monde et le Test du Village Imaginaire.* Paris: Presses Universitaires de France, 1960.
Because of its importance, this reference in French is the sole ex-ception in this "English-only" bibliography. We are grateful to Robert Royeton for making available to us a translation of the first two chapters, which are the definitive work on the historical background of the sandtray world and its derivatives, and which are available through the library of the C. G. Jung Institute of San Francisco.

Pickford, Ruth. The versatility of the World Technique. *Projective Psychology,* 1973, *18,* 21-23.

The best short overview of Lowenfeld's World Technique. As the title implies, the method is looked at from many different points of view.

Stewart, Louis H. Sandplay therapy: Jungian technique. In B. B. Wolman (Ed.) *International Encylopedia of psychiatry, psychology, psychoanalysis, and neurology.* New York: Aesculapius Publishers, 1977, Vol. 10, 9-11.
Traces the introduction of sandplay into Jungian analysis, some fifty years after Jung first engaged in similar activity in his own self-analysis. Its therapeutic value is seen in the link it provides with the play world of children, still present in the adult.

Stone, Lawrence J. The Toy World Test. In O. K. Buros (Ed.), *The Fifth Mental Measurements Yearbook.* Highland Park, New Jersey: The Gryphon Press, 1959, 168-169.
A thoughtful and considered evaluation of Bühler's World Test, which finds it to compare favorably with other projective techniques. One important omission in the test's standardization is pointed out.

Sullwold, Edith. Eagle eye. In H. Kirsch (Ed.), *The well-tended tree.* New York: G. P. Putnam's Sons, 1971, 235-252.
The treatment of a boy by a Jungian-oriented therapist, using sandplay among other methods. Better than almost any published case we know, this makes clear exactly how sandplay fits into the total therapeutic picture, rather than isolating it for consideration.

Sullwold, Edith. Jungian child therapy. In B. B. Wolman (Ed.), *International Encyclopedia of psychiatry, psycholgy, psychoanalysis, and neurology.* New York: Aesculapius Publishers, 1977, Vol. 6, 242-246.
A short overview of developmental stages and of the indications for therapy with children. Methods, including fantasy, are considered from a Jungian point of view. Fits very well with the case of Eagle Eye as an introduction to child therapy.

Wells, H[erbert] G[eorge]. *Floor Games*. New York: Arno Press, 1975.
This delightful volume appears to be a reproduction of the 1912 Boston edition. According to the summary it "suggests some of the games that can be created using toy soldiers and other figurines, blocks, boards and planks, and toy trains arranged in various ways on an appropriate floor." Although the writer's comments on the constructions are nonpsychological, the rapport with his two sons during his participation in this activity is evident. In his 1913 *Little Wars* (New York: Da Capo Press, 1977) Wells refers to himself as author of "*Floor Games* and several minor and inferior works."

# Appendix
# Bibliography of Works
# on Standardization

★ *Also appears in the Annotated Bibliography*

Allan, John, and Patricia Berry. "Sandplay." Special issue: Counseling with Expressive Arts. In *Elementary School Guidance and Couseling,* 21: 4, 300–306, April 1987

Bolgar, Hedda, and Liselotte Fischer. The Toy Test: A Psychodiagnostic Method." In *Psychological Bulletin,* 37: 517–518, 1940

★Bolgar, Hedda, and Liselotte Fischer. "Personality Projection in the World Test." In *American Journal of Orthopsychiatry,* 17: 117–128, 1947

★Bowyer, Laura Ruth. "The Importance of Sand in the World Technique: An Experiment." In *British Journal of Educational Psychology,* 29: 162–164, 1959

★Bowyer, Laura Ruth. *The Lowenfeld World Technique.* Oxford: Pergamon Press, 1970

Bradway, Katherine. *Sandplay Bridges and the Transcendent Function.* San Francisco: The C.G. Jung Institute, 1985

Bradway, Katherine. "Sandplay: What Makes it Work?" In Mary Ann Mattoon, Ed., *Proceedings of the Tenth International Congress of Analytical Psychology.* Einsiedeln, Switzerland: Daimon Verlag, 1987

Bühler, Charlotte. "Symbolic Action in Children." In *New York Academy of Sciences. Transactions.* 1941, II, 4, 63

Bühler, Charlotte. "The World Test." In *Journal of Child Psychiatry,* 2, 1: 2–3, 1951(a)

Bühler, Charlotte. "The World Test, A Projective Technique." In *Journal of Child Psychiatry*, 2, 1: 4-23, 1951(b)

*Bühler, Charlotte. "The World Test. Manual of Directions." In *Journal of Child Psychiatry*, 2, 1: 69-81, 1951(c)

Bühler, Charlotte. "National Differences in 'World Test' Projective Patterns." In *Journal of Projective Techniques*, 16: 42-55, 1952

Bühler, Charlotte, and Helen Sara Carroll. "A Comparison of the Results of the World Test with Teachers' Judgments Concerning Children's Personality Adjustment. In *Journal of Child Psychiatry*, 2, 1:36-68, 1951

Bühler, Charlotte, and G. Kelley. *The World Test: A Measurement of Emotional Disturbance*. New York: The Psychological Corporation, 1941 (Replaced by Bühler and Carroll, 1951, above)

Ferrier, M.J. "Use of Projective Methods in Analytic Psychotherapy." In *Annales Medico-Psychologiques*, 2, 109, 1968

Fischer, Liselotte. "A New Psychological Tool in Function: Preliminary Clinical Experience with the Bolgar-Fischer World Test." In *American Journal of Orthopsychiatry*, 20: 281-292, 1950

*Fujii, Shinobu. "Retest Reliability of the Sandplay Technique (First Report)." In *British Journal of Projective Psychology and Personality Study*, 24:21-25, 1979

Gillies, John. "Personality and Adjustment in Deaf Children." In *British Journal of Projective Psychology and Personality Study*, 20, 1: 33-34, June 1975

Kamp, J.M.J., and E.S. Kessler. "The World Test: Developmental Aspects of a Play Technique." In *Journal of Child Psychology and Psychiatry and Applied Disciplines*, 11: 81-108, 1970 (Also appeared in French in *Revue de Neuropsychiatrie Infantile et d'Hygiene Mentale de l'Enfance*, 19: 295-322, 1971)

*Lowenfeld, Margaret. "The World Technique." In *Topical Problems in Psychotherapy*. 3: 248-263, 1960

Lumry, Gayle Kelley. "Study of World Test Characteristics as a Basis for Discrimination Between Various Clinical Categories." In *Journal of Child Psychiatry*, 2, 1: 24-35, 1951

Michael, Joseph C., and Charlotte Bühler. "Experiences with Personality Testing in a Neuropsychiatric Department of a Public

General Hospital." In *Diseases of the Nervous System,* 7: 205–211, 1945

Noyes, Mary. "Sandplay Imagery: An Aid to Teaching Reading." In *Academic Therapy,* 17, 2: 231–237, November 1981

Pascal, Gerald R. "Gestalt Functions: The Bender–Gestalt, Mosaic, and World Tests." In Daniel Brower and Lawrence E. Abt, Eds., *Progress in Clinical Psychology,* Vol. I, Section 1, pp. 185–191. New York: Grune and Stratton, 1952

Ryce-Menuhin, Joel. "Sandplay in an Adult Jungian Psychotherapy." In *British Journal of Projective Psychology and Personality Study,* 28, 2: 13–21, December 1983

Stewart, Louis H. "Sandplay in Analysis." In Murray Stein, Ed., *Jungian Analysis.* Wilmette, IL: Open Court, 1982

*Stone, L.J. "The Toy World Test." In O.K. Buros, Ed., *The Fifth Mental Measurements Yearbook.* Highland Park, NJ: The Gryphon Press, 1959, pp. 168–169

Ucko, L.E. "Early Stress Experiences Mirrored in World Play Test at Five Years." In *Human Development,* 10: 107–127, 1967

Weinrib, Estelle. *Images of the Self.* Boston: Sigo Press, 1983

Weinrib, Estelle. "The Shadow and the Cross." In Mary Ann Mattoon, Ed., *Proceedings of the Tenth International Congress of Analytical Psychology.* Einsiedeln, Switzerland: Daimon Verlag, 1987

## Dissertations:

Carmody, John. "Self-Restoration and Initiation in Analytical Child Therapy: Observations on Sandplay." Ph.D. dissertation, Saybrook Institute, 1984. Dissertation Abstracts International, 45, 8: 2681, February 1985. University Microfilms Order Number ADG84-25701

Crable, Pauline G. "Women and Self: An Initial Investigation of the Feminine Essence Using Sandplay." Dissertation Abstracts International, 37, 3B: 1483, September 1976. University Microfilms Order Number ADG76-19751

Denkers, Glory. "An Investigation of the Diagnostic Potential of Sandplay Utilizing Linn Jones' Developmental Scoring System." Ph.D. dissertation, Psychological Studies Institute, 1985

Domenico, Gisela Schuback. "The Lowenfeld World Apparatus: A Methodological Contribution Towards the Study and the Analysis of the Sand Tray Process."

# Index

234 INDEX

Elephant figures, 138–39, 176–77
Eleventh International Congress of
  Psychology (1937), 8
Energy, 61, 160–61, 196, 208; in
  children's sandtrays, 94, 96, 97–99;
  in men's sandtrays, 170, 173, 177; in
  women's sandtrays, 143, 147–48, 149
Equilibration, 29, 30, 35–36, 48–49,
  61, 129
Erikson, Erik: developmental theory
  of, 46–48, 50, 54, 57, 61, 72;
  preadolescent play and, 8–9, 17,
  83–84; sandtray techniques of, 10–11,
  14, 19
Eros, 111, 130, 138
Eternal Child, 21, 29, 35–37
Ethnic figures, 105, 128, 177–78. *See
  also* American Indian figures
Expressive profile, 40, 70, 92, 140
Extraversion, 34, 114, 158, 181, 183; in
  sandtray, 116, 129

Fantasy, 13, 29, 36, 43, 49, 128; Jung
  and, 30–35; therapeutic containment
  and, 19, 120, 136
"Fantasy, Dreams and Myths"
  (Berkeley), 2
Fantasy play, 49, 73
Farm animal figures. *See* Domestic
  animal figures
Farm scenes, 86–89, 97–98
Father archetype: in children's
  · development, 70, 85, 93; in men's
  development, 106–21 *passim*, 130,
  159, 163, 169–84 *passim*, 193–94
Father complex, 101, 110, 157, 159,
  160n
Father-son relationship, 110–20 *passim*,
  158–59, 170–74, 184, 188–89
Feather, 106, 170, 178, 191
Feeling function, 34, 129, 200; in men,
  120–21, 158; in women, 137–38,
  147–48
Female figures: in children's sandtrays,
  63, 67–68, 76, 83, 90, 95–99; in
  men's sandtrays, 106, 163, 174–79,
  185–86, 193, 194; in women's

sandtrays, 139–52 *passim*, 201–3, 205
Feminine principle: in children's
  sandtrays, 95, 98; in men's
  sandtrays, 111, 130, 159–61, 164, 172;
  in women's sandtrays, 138–40, 144,
  148, 150, 154
Fences, in sandtray, 12, 89, 96–97, 165
Fight-flight pattern, 71
Fighting stage, 93, 95–96
Figurative play, 59
Fischer, Liselotte, 9
Fish, game of, 68
Flavell, John H., 54–55
Flight syndrome, 71
*Floor Games* (Wells), 5–6, 21, 27–29
Food, in sandtray, 73, 94, 97–98
Fool, 130
Fordham, Michael, 8
"Forgotten Feminine, The"
  (Berkeley), 2
Found objects, for sandtray, 105, 134
Freud, Sigmund, 31, 47, 102, 109,
  160–61
Functions, of ego, 33–34. *See also
  specific functions*
Furniture, 84

Game preference scales, 84–85
Games, 39–40, 43n, 44, 51–52; in Early
  Childhood I, 52–53, 59–69, 71, 74,
  76; in Early Childhod II, 53, 70–82;
  in Infancy, 53, 54–59; in Middle
  Childhood, 53, 68, 83–86; rules in,
  68, 72–73, 85–86; sex differences in,
  83–85, 86; theory of, 52–53
Gargoyle figure, 176–77
Garner, Ann Margaret, 6–7
Gasoline station, in sandtray, 99
Gates, in sandtray, 12, 89
Geisha figure, 147, 148, 152
Geometrical shapes, 126; in children's
  sandtrays, 59; in men's sandtrays,
  108, 121–22, 176; in women's
  sandtrays, 152, 155
Girl figures, 83, 97–98, 144, 147,
  150–52
Gods, figures of, 190–91